Corporate Financial Decisions
and Market Value

Contributions to Management Science

Giovanni Marseguerra

Corporate Financial Decisions and Market Value

Studies on Dividend Policy, Price Volatility, and Ownership Structure

With 17 Figures

Physica-Verlag

A Springer-Verlag Company

Series Editors
Werner A. Müller
Peter Schuster

Author
Dr. Giovanni Marseguerra
Università Cattolica del Sacro Cuore
Istituto di Econometria e Matematica
Largo Gemelli 1
I-20123 Milano, Italy

ISBN 3-7908-1047-9 Physica-Verlag Heidelberg New York

Cataloging-in-Publication Data applied for
Die Deutsche Bibliothek – CIP-Einheitsaufnahme
Marseguerra, Giovanni: Corporate financial decisions and market value: studies on dividend policy, price volatility, and ownership structure / Giovanni Marseguerra. – Heidelberg: Physica-Verl., 1998
  (Contributions to management science)
  ISBN 3-7908-1047-9

© Physica-Verlag Heidelberg 1998
Printed in Germany

Softcover Design: Erich Kirchner, Heidelberg

SPIN 10637948   88/2202-5 4 3 2 1 0 – Printed on acid-free paper

Preface

How do managers of a firm choose between alternative financial policies? Can the choice of a particular financial policy affect the value of the firm? Since the early 1960s, the debate on these questions has been lively and interesting as economists have investigated the effect on the value of the firm of relaxing the various assumptions in the celebrated Modigliani-Miller theory. Furthermore, even if we stick to the MM-assumptions (that is, we assume perfect and complete capital markets, no taxes and symmetric information), and we therefore know that only optimally chosen investments determine firm's value, another interesting question arises: How does the structure of ownership affect investment decisions (and, in turn, values)? This research monograph attempts to analyze some of the issues involved in this debate. It belongs to the area of mathematical economics and is intended to appeal to mathematical economists as well as economists and mathematicians. It is meant to deal with economically relevant problems in a mathematically adequate way. To decide whether or not it succeeds in this task, it is up to the reader.

I am greatly indebted to Dr. Margaret Bray for her supervision of my PhD thesis in Economics at the London School of Economics from which this book resulted. She helped me as friend and adviser through many struggles in the last three years and invested a great amount of work in this thesis. Besides, Chapters 5 and 6 of the book are based on joint ongoing research. I learnt (and I am still learning) a lot from her.

I wish also to thank the examiners for my PhD degree, Professors Julian Franks and Ailsa Roell, for their insightful comments which led me to improve the thesis in several respects.

I am especially grateful to Professors Pier Carlo Nicola and Alberto Quadrio Curzio for their continuous guidance, encouragement and support. They first aroused my interest for Economic Theory and I owe a great debt of gratitude to them.

I would also like to thank Professor Mario Faliva. His supportive attitude towards my work was a great help.

I owe thanks to Enrico Bellino, Francesco Brioschi, Luigi Buzzacchi, Gianluca Femminis, Guido Merzoni, Espen Moen, Stefano Paleari, Carlos Velasco, Gerd Weinrich and Paolo Zaffaroni for many helpful discussions.

At various stages of my research at LSE I have received financial support from Fondazione Einaudi di Torino, Mediocredito Centrale ("Marco Fanno" scholarship) and Consiglio Nazionale delle Ricerche. I am indebted to all of them.

I would like to express my gratitude to my family who gave me the possibilities to do what I wanted. They were a continuous source of encouragement.

At last, but certainly not least, I want to thank my wife Elena for her support and understanding, first during my PhD research and then during the preparation of this monograph. Without her help the book could not have been written.

There is someone to whom I owe more than thanks. I would like to dedicate this book to her.

Table of Contents

Introduction

One major theme in the theory of finance during the last three decades has been the analysis (both at theoretical and empirical level) of whether (and how) a firm's financial policy decision is able to affect its overall valuation. For example, can any financing decision affect the value of the firm? Moreover, is shareholders' wealth affected by the dividend policy of the firm? Both these decisions are widely regarded by corporate finance directors, investors and market participants as issues of considerable importance. And yet the classical theoretical articles on the subject (Modigliani and Miller, 1958, and Miller and Modigliani, 1961) conclude, under rather restrictive assumptions, that both these decisions (i.e., the choice of firm's capital structure and dividend policy) are irrelevant. The essence of the MM proof is that, in a world of perfect and complete markets in which taxation and asymmetric information are absent, investors can, from one hand, create their *home-made dividends* by selling shares of stock, and from the other engage in *home-made leverage* by borrowing on their own account. Thus, shareholders are indifferent to both the amount of debt in the capital structure and the dividend policy of their firm. As a consequence, the value of the firm is independent of its capital structure and of its dividend policy. The striking contrast between theory and practice has led to careful (and critical) examinations of the assumptions of the MM theory. Many (rather sophisticated) models have appeared in the literature, and some progress has been made in identifying ways in which dividend policy and capital structure may matter. But the determinants of firms' debt and dividend policies are not yet fully understood. Moreover, in part as a consequence of the empirical observation of the striking differences in patterns of corporate ownership in industrialized countries, another question has recently started to puzzle financial economists: How does a firm's ownership structure affect value? Even casual empiricism shows that changes in property rights affect managers' behaviour, and so, presumably, investments. Thus, firm's value has to depend on ownership structure. But how? The debate on this matter is, in some sense, even at an earlier stage than that on capital structure and dividend policy.

Questions like those mentioned above motivate this research monograph. The book deals with several aspects of the impact of corporate financial policy decisions on market value. The 11 Chapters that follow are divided into three major parts. Part I, "Markets and Information" (Chapters 1 through 3) moves away from the classical MM framework by relaxing the assumption of symmetric information between firm's managers and market's participants and analyzes (through the derivation of a formal mathematical model) a number of theoretical perspectives on the topic of the transmission of information through dividend policy. Part II, "Managers and Stock Price" (Chapters 4 through 6) is devoted to analyze the effects of dividend policy on stock price when markets are efficient by assumption. The analysis is concerned chiefly with the issue of the supposed excess stock price volatility. Moreover, the interrelation between prices' volatility and dividends' volatility is investigated. Part III, "Ownership and Investments" (Chapters 7 through 11) aims to analyze the effects of ownership structure on the internal efficiency of firms. The analysis is mainly concerned with the business group form of corporate ownership. Alternative forms of within group capital allocation decisions are presented and compared. The analysis is then extended to the links between ownership and forms of corporate governance.

We commence in Chapter 1 with a review of the existing alternative theories of why dividend policy may matter in a world where some of the MM assumptions fail to be satisfied and we focus, in particular, on the relation of dividends to information. Chapter 2 investigates the information content of dividends in a dynamic setting with learning. Asymmetric information between managers and shareholders of a publicly traded firm is modelled by means of a state variable (*the prosperity* of the firm) unobservable to the market. The latter, however, can make inference through dividends and earnings, which are a noisy observation of the state variable. This inference mechanism is modelled by means of a standard Kalman filter. It is shown that, under rather general assumptions, convergence of the learning procedure is guaranteed. The analysis is extended in Chapter 3 to take into account the effects of publicly available information on the market's inference procedure. It is shown that the information contained in dividend announcements, as measured by the reduction in the market's uncertainty on the true state of the firm, depends crucially on the amount of information already available to the market.

Chapter 4 sets out basic issues relevant to the analysis of price movements in speculative markets and reviews the principal results which have emerged from the long standing debate on the presumed excess volatility of stock prices. Chapter 5 investigates the relationship between dividend policy and stock price in an efficient market. It is shown how there is a fundamental trade-off between volatility in prices and volatility in dividends, so that managers' dividend smoothing policies effectively exploit this trade-off. In Chapter 6 the volatility of stock prices is analyzed within a framework sufficiently flexible to handle both conditions of stationarity and non stationarity. The conditions leading to *gross* violations of the variance bound inequality are fully characterized. The results of numerical simulations clearly show that the economy in the model easily reproduces plots similar to those used by Shiller (1981) to claim the failure of the efficient market hypothesis, even when prices and dividends are stationary.

Chapter 7 is devoted to present the basic mathematical model which will be used in the rest of the book to define the concepts of value and ownership in a market characterized by equity linkages between firms. Chapter 8 analyzes the influence of ownership structure on investment allocation decisions in a hierarchical corporate group. Resource allocation processes in both a group and a multidivisional firm are analyzed and compared. Conditions on the (integrated) group's ownership structure are established which make the multidivisional form preferable for minority shareholders. The effect of changes in ownership structure on both the underlying and market values of the group's member firms are also analyzed. In Chapter 9 is then presented a numerical example in which the relation between ownership and investmnts is easily spelled out. The role of institutional investors in industrialized countries in the light of the experience accumulated in recent years is assessed in Chapter 10 and, finally, the implications for corporate governance of institutional investor activism are examined in Chapter 11 which concludes the monograph.

Part I

Markets and Information

Chapter 1

The Information Content of Dividends

1.1 Introduction

The seminal contribution to research on dividend policy is Miller and Modigliani (1961). They show that with complete and perfect capital markets and no taxes, a firm's dividend policy will not affect its value. The basic premise of their argument is that firm value is determined by choosing optimal investments. The firm net payout, defined as the difference between earnings and investments, is simply a residual. Since the net payout consists of dividends and shares issues/repurchases, a firm can always adjust its dividends to any level with an offsetting change in shares outstanding. Financing an increased dividend by issuing new equity or decreasing dividends by repurchasing equity merely involves a transfer of ownership, the underlying cash flow to securityholders is unchanged and so the value of the firm is unchanged. Dividend policy is also irrelevant for investors, because any desired stream of payments can be replicated by appropriate purchases and sales of equity. However, if dividend policy is essentially an exercise of financial packaging, if dividends are simply a financial detail, why are announcements of dividend increases typically followed by stock price increases, sometimes spectacularly so? Why are dividend cuts or elimination often followed by price falls, sometimes even more spectacular? [1]

---

[1] Merton Miller happened to be lecturing on the dividend irrelevance proposition to the research department of a large Wall Steet brokerage firm in December 1958 at the very moment when the American Telephone and Telegraph Corporation announced an increase in the annual level of dividend it had maintained for the previous thirty years. And when trading (and his lecture on dividend irrelevance) was resumed a half-hour later, A.T.&T. had jumped in price by over 10% (see Miller, 1987).

1.1.1 Asymmetric Information

One of the assumptions characterizing perfect capital markets is symmetric information. i.e. everything relevant to valuation known by the firm's managers must also be known to the investing public. Unfortunately this condition is in practice very seldom satisfied and, in particular, if at the time of the dividend announcement managers know more about firm's future prospects than investors, the latter may interpret an announced increase in dividends as a sign of improved prospects for the firm's earnings (higher dividends being associated with higher future earnings). This was in fact the explanation of the observed empirical evidence given by Miller and Modigliani in their original article. They suggested that if management's expectations of future earnings affect their decision about current dividend payouts, then changes in dividends will convey information to the market about future earnings And it is to this improved real earnings prospect rather than to the dividend increase per se that the market is responding. The effects of management's dividend decisions on the value of the firm may be clearly envisioned in this quotation from Merton Miller, 1986, p.302:

> "As the date for announcing the regular quarterly dividend approaches, the market forms an expectation of what the dividend will be. This expectation is based on the market's estimates of the firm's earnings, investment opportunities and financing plans. These estimates are, in turn, based on information the market has about the state of the economy, the industry, the firm's past dividend decisions, changes in the tax trade-offs, and so on. If the actual announced dividend is just what the market expected, then there may be no price movement at all, even if the announced dividend is larger than the previous one. It was expected to be larger, and was fully discounted long ago. But if the announced dividend is higher than the market was expecting, then the market will start rethinking its appraisal".

The notion that changes in dividends can convey information to the market about future earnings has been labelled *the informa-tion content of dividends*. As we will discuss below (see §1.2), this notion has been formalized in two ways: Dividends may be used either as an ex-ante signal of future cash flow (as, for example, in Bhattacharya, 1979), or they may provide information about earnings as a description of the sources and uses of funds identity (as, for example, in Miller and Rock, 1985). It is important to rec-ognize that the fact that dividends convey information does not necessarily imply that they are being used as a signal, as they may not be consciously set to convey information. Indeed, the analy-sis in this Part of the book addresses the issue of the information content of dividends from the perspective of a simple transmission of information. We assume asymmetric information between the managers of a publicly traded firm and the shareholders in the market. This asymmetry of information is modelled by means of a state variable which is intended to represent the prosperity of the firm. Managers know the realization of this random variable and set dividends in a way which (among other things) depend on this realization. The market, on the contrary, cannot observe the value of the state variable directly. It can, however, make inference through dividends, which are a noisy observation of the state variable. This inference mechanism is modelled in Chapter 2 by means of a standard Kalman filter which enables the market to compute an estimate of the true state of the firm.

1.1.2 Public Information

Chapter 3 will be devoted to the analysis of how the above described market inference mechanism is affected by the publicly available information. The market receives a large amount of in-formation concerning the value of the firm's state variable. This comes from official publications, from stockbrokers' advice, and other sources. We can also think of the firm as publicly and vol-untarily disclosing information about the state variable. All this information, from whatever source it comes, affects the market's perception of firm's prospects, and the information content of div-idends depends upon what is already known about the firm before the announcement. There is a large body of literature (see, e.g.,

Diamond, 1985) which analyzes how the market reacts to information released by firms (e.g. the quantity of costly information that
the shareholders decide to acquire before making their investment
decisions) but this framework fudges the question of the simul-
taneous transmission of information through publicly observable
financial decisions (e.g. dividends). We examine instead the relationship between these two pieces of noisy information available
on the market, namely the *open information*, obtained through
(friendly or paid for) advice, public announcements, and press
releases, and the *hidden information*, contained in the publicly
observable financial decisions. Only when the two parts of the
story are simultaneously considered it is possible to analyze in an
appropriate way the empirical evidence of large stock price reactions to dividend announcements.

1.1.3 Overview of Part I

The rest of Part I is organized as follows. In section 1.2, after
briefly reviewing some theoretical and empirical facts concerning
the informative role of dividends, it will be argued that the information in dividend announcements may be very different for
different *boundary conditions* (i.e. what people do know about
the announcing corporation). This analysis should motivate the
subsequent research. In Chapter 2 using a simple Kalman filter
technique the process of signal extraction from dividends is studied in a very simplified framework with no extra information available to the market except that contained in dividends. Chapter 3
examines how the market inference mechanism is affected by the
publicly available information. Some final remarks and possible
extensions conclude this Part of the book .

1.2 Dividends and Information

As mentioned in the Introduction, in their seminal contribution Miller and Modigliani (1961) showed that with complete and
perfect capital markets and with no personal or corporate taxes,

firms cannot alter their value by changing dividend policy. Dividend policy therefore can only affect value when (at least) one of the assumptions underlying the irrelevance proposition is violated. In particular, perfect and complete capital markets have the following elements (Allen and Michaely, 1994):

  i) No taxes
 ii) Symmetric information (i.e. all the investors have the same informations, and investors have the same information as the managers)
iii) Complete contracting possibilities (i.e. there are no contracting or agency costs associated with stock ownership)
 iv) No transaction costs (i.e. when a) individuals buy and sell securities and b) firms issue and repurchase shares, both operations are costlessly)
  v) Complete markets

Let us briefly examine the role played by each of the above assumptions. As far as assumption i) is concerned, notice that, if dividends and shares repurchases are taxed differently, it is no longer irrelevant whether a firm pays out dividends or repurchases shares. For example, if dividends are taxed at a higher rate than capital gains from shares repurchases (as it has been the case in the U.S. until the 1986 Tax Reform Act), then it is optimal for the firm to pay no dividends and instead to pay out any residual funds by repurchasing shares [2]. Assumption ii) is very rarely satisfied since managers are likely to know more about the current

---

[2] In the U.S., after the 1986 Tax Reform Act, dividends and capital gains are taxed at the same rate. However, taxes on dividends have to be paid immediately, while taxes on capital gains can be deferred until shares are sold and capital gains are realized. Moreover, many financial institutions (e.g., pension funds) operate free of all taxes, and therefore have no reason to prefer capital gains to dividends, or vice versa. Only corporations have a tax reason to prefer dividends, since they pay corporate income tax on only 30 per cent of any dividend received. In the UK under the imputation system of corporate taxation tax exempt investors (as, e.g., pension funds) benefit from dividends, which enable them to reclaim Advance Corporation Tax.

and future prospects of the firm than outside investors. Dividens may then reveal some information to outsiders about firm's value. Furthermore, dividends may also be used by managers to change the market's perception about firm's true value. In both cases, dividend policy may therefore affect value. If assumption iii) were to hold, it would be possible to motivate the managers' decisions through the use of forcing contracts. However, without complete contracting possibilities, dividend policy could be used to force managers to act in the interests of shareholders (e.g., high dividends might discipline managerial behaviour). This in turn would raise firm value. Both transaction costs incurred by investors when selling securities and making decisions about such sales, and flotation costs incurred by firms when they tap the capital market with equity issues make assumption iv) untenable in almost any circumstances. Dividend payments might therefore be the cheapest way for investors to achieve a steady flow of income from their capital investment (and, again, dividend policy would affect value). Finally, if markets were incomplete, marginal rates of substitution between current and future consumption might vary across consumers/investors so that firms might be able to increase value by adjusting their dividend policies in order to attract a particular group of investors.

In this part of the book, contrary to the MM assumption that investors have the same informations as mangers, we will assume that capital markets are informationally imperfect. As already mentioned, the information content of dividends hypothesis (originally suggested by Miller and Modigliani, 1961) is based on the assumption that managers possess more information about the prospects of the firm than individuals outside the firms. The hypothesis asserts that dividend changes convey manager's inside information to outsiders and has its roots in Lintner's (1956) classic study on dividend policy. Lintner interviewed a sample of corporate managers. One of the primary findings of the interviews is that a high proportion of managers attempt to maintain a stable regular dividend and dividend paying firms increase their dividends only when management is relatively confident that the higher payments can be maintained [3]. Lintner (1956) also found a time-series relation between annual dividends and earnings that is consistent with this view. Additional empirical support to Lintner's argument was provided by Fama and Babiak, (1968), and DeAngelo and DeAngelo, (1989).

If managers change regular dividends only when the earnings potential of the firm has changed, changes in regular dividends are likely to provide some information to the market about the firm's prospects. However, was only towards the end of 1970s that formal models of dividends and information signalling were developed. If the marginal cost of paying dividends decreases with the market's undervaluation of the firm, and if managers care about the current share price, then Spence (1973) signaling equilibria may exist. Managers with favourable information reveal it by initiating or increasing dividends, whereas the same dividend signal is prohibitively costly for managers without favourable information. Separating costs that establish signalling equilibria include personal taxes (Bhattacharya, 1979), sub-optimal investment (Miller and Rock, 1985) and ownership dilution along with personal taxes (John and Williams, 1985). However, as Allen and Michaely (1994) point out, dividends may convey informations to the market without necessarily being used by the managers as a signal. The distinction may be subtle but is crucially important in interpreting the empirical tests as supporting the signalling theory since the empirical tests we are aware of cannot help us in distinguishing between these two alternatives. There are essentially three implications of the information/signalling hypothesis which have been empirically tested. They are, of course, only necessary but insufficient conditions for the hypothesis to hold. The first implication is that dividend changes should be positively associated with subsequent earning changes. This condition is extremely important since, if it is not met, we may conclude that dividends do not even have the potential to transmit information,

---

[3] In Lintner's words, managers usually demonstrate a "reluctance (common to all companies) to reduce regular rates once established and a consequent conservatism in raising regular rates" (Lintner, 1956, p.84)

let alone the signal. Unfortunately, the overall accumulated evidence (Watts, 1973, Gonedes, 1978) grants only weak support to the assertion that dividend changes convey information about future changes in earnings, unless extreme dividend changes are considered (as in Healy and Palepu, 1988). The second empirically tested implication of the information/signalling hypothesis is that unexpected changes in dividends should be followed by revisions in the market's expectations of future earnings in the same direction as the dividend change. Ofer and Siegel (1987) find that knowledge of dividend announcements does improve the accuracy of the average analyst's preannouncement forecasts of future earnings. Moreover, they find that analysts revise their earnings forecast by an amount that is positively related to the size of the announced dividend change. The third implication of the information/signalling hypothesis is that unexpected dividend changes should be positively associated to stock price changes. The evidence supports this prediction almost uniformly [4]. There are several empirical studies (Fama-Fisher-Jensen and Roll, 1969, Pettit, 1972) which show that the announcements of dividend increases are followed by a significant price increase, and announcements of dividend decreases are followed by a significant price drop. Moreover, Ahavony and Swary (1980) show that these relationships hold even after controlling for contemporaneous earnings

---

[4] Notice that a positive association between announcements of dividend changes and stock price movements is also consistent with the free cash flow/overinvestment explanation of why firms pay dividends of Jensen (1986), who argues that a firm with substantial free cash flow will have a tendency to overinvest by accepting investment projects with negative net present values. If managers are overinvesting, an increase in dividends will, other things being equal, reduce the extent of overinvestment and increase the market value of the firm, and a decrease in the dividends will have the opposite result. Jensen views the empirical evidence of a positive association between dividend change announcement and stock price movements as supporting the free cash flow hypothesis. A recent empirical analysis (Lang and Litzenberger, 1989) also seems to support the overinvestment hypothesis over the signalling hypothesis.

announcements.

In summary, the empirical evidence is far from conclusive, since the relationship between dividend changes and subsequent earnings changes is positive but not significant. Several empirical studies indicate that announcements of dividend changes do convey information to the market. However, the question of precisely what information is contained in dividend announcements has not been fully resolved. For example, do dividend cuts always signal bad news? Under certain conditions it can be argued that the signal sent to the market by a dividend cut is a positive one, the opposite of that posited by the traditional dividend information hypothesis. Specifically, if a company has many profitable investment opportunities, but little available cash, and if the cost of external financing is substantial, the value of that company's share may be increased by reducing current dividends and increasing investments. At the same time, if a company has a limited supply of profitable investment opportunities, shareholders may be better off if the excess cash is paid out to them in the form of higher dividends. In both of these situations, the signal sent to the market about internal investment opportunities and prospective company performances would be the opposite of that predicted by the conventional models of dividend changes; under this alternative hypothesis, dividend increases signal reduced investment opportunities and lower future earnings, while dividend cuts are interpreted as signs of favourable opportunities. Woolridge and Gosh (1986) explore this alternative dividend information hypothesis and present some supporting empirical data on companies cutting their dividends. They argue that if investment opportunities exist and if external financing is costly, stockholders' wealth may be increased by management's decision to reduce cash dividends to provide lower cost funding for new investment. Under such circumstances, a dividend cut accompanied by some alternative but effective signal of future growth opportunities [5] could convey positive information to the market, resulting in an increase, not a

---

[5] In the examples provided by Woolridge and Gosh this alternative signal is mainly represented by a public disclosure of these investment opportunities (e.g. by means of press releases).

decline, in stock price. [6]

This discussion indicates that the market's knowledge of the firm's prospects before the dividend announcements affect the information content of dividends. It seems reasonable to assume that the latter depends upon the quality and quantity of information available to the market at the moment of the announcement. A recent empirical analysis (Bajaj and Vijh, 1990) seems to support this hypothesis. Bajaj and Vijh find that price reactions to dividend changes are higher for small firm stocks. Their conjecture is that the greater price reaction for small firm stocks indicates that their dividend announcements convey more information, "perhaps because less information is produced for such firms in other periods" (Bajaj and Vijh, p.196).

Wang, 1994, addresses the issue of the transmission of information through dividends from a perspective which is very close to that developed in this Chapter. He derives a model of competitive stock trading in which investors are heterogeneous in their information and private investment opportunities. In the Wang's model the underlying state variables of the economy are a persistent component of dividends and the expected excess rate of return from a risky production technology available to informed investors. The former determines the stock's future cash flow and the latter determines the private investment opportunity. Under asymmetric information the equilibrium depends not only on the true values of the underlying state variables but also on the uninformed investors' expectations of these variables. Since the latter are not publicly observable, the uninformed investor rationally extract information about their values based on realized dividends, prices and public signals. The focus of the Wang's paper, however, is on the link between the nature of the heterogeneity among investors and the behaviour of trading volume (and its relation to price dynamics) and the issue of the extraction of information from dividends is only marginally addressed.

Firms, particularly quoted firms, are subject to close market's scrutiny. Investment analysts offer advice to individuals and

---

[6] This proposition has not been tested, but a similar issue has been addressed by Divecha and Morse (1983).

institutions as specific buy, sell or hold recommendations or as financial forecasts of earnings and dividends. Financial data are also available from government statistics, and from commercial firms that specialize in disseminating financial data. Moreover, publicly traded firms devote a substantial part of their resources to releasing information to outside investors. This is particularly true on dates when the firm is selling new securities: firstly because there are regulatory requirements to do so [7], and secondly because of the well known adverse selection problem (see ,e.g., Myers and Majluf (1984)). But firms release information on an almost continuous basis. Prospectuses, circulars and offer documents are issued by firms to their actual and potential shareholders under a number of circumstances and the actual content is regulated by a variety of sources depending on the specific case [8]. There are several reasons to explain this disclosure of information. Interim accounting statements are required in many countries from larger or publicly quoted firms. These may be quarterly, as in the US, or half-yearly as in the UK. While the content of these releases is extremely modest, as they may contain little more than turnover, profit, tax, dividends and earnings per share, their impact is invaluable.

The information released may help financial markets to value

---

[7] In the United States the issuance of new securities is regulated by the SEC under Security Act of 1933. The issuing firm is required to provide a minimum amount of information about the firm, its business environment and its financial condition so that investors can value the firm.

[8] The models on disclosure regulation in financial markets with asymmetric information (e.g. Diamond (1985), Verrecchia (1983)) usually assume that misrepresentation of the information produced by the firm is not possible, i.e. it is ruled out by prohibitively high potential penalties for fraud. Such a no–misrepresentation postulate assumes in effect not only that some governmental enforcement mechanism with prohibitively high penalties for detected lies exists, but also that lies can be perfectly distinguished from true telling with non zero probability (for further discussion related to this point, see Beales, Craswell and Salop, 1981).

the firm accurately. Managers may therefore be induced to consider voluntary disclosure as a mechanism to eliminate or reduce
information asymmetries between themselves and external par-
ties [9]. Also, more efficient firm's security prices can lead to more
efficient investment decisions. This may provide firms with the
incentive to increase price efficiency by voluntarily disclosing information (see, e.g., Fishman and Hagerty (1989)).

Diamond (1985) uses a noisy competitive Rational Expectations Equilibrium model with diverse information to demonstrate
that there exists a policy of disclosure of information which makes
all shareholders better off than a policy of no disclosure. The
welfare improvement occurs mainly because some traders would
acquire costly information in the absence of the public announcement, while all abstain from information collection given the announcement. However, it is not clear what people would have
done if a financial decision was also observable and used to draw
inferences about the firm's future prospects. This inference mechanism is the subject of the next Chapter.

---

[9] It is not clear, however, when this is in manager's interests.

Chapter 2

An Application of the Kalman Filter

In this Chapter we address the issue of the information transmission through dividends in a simplified framework making use of a standard Kalman filter technique. As mentioned above (see §1.2), while it seems empirically evident that dividend changes do convey information to the market, nonetheless is still not clear exactly what information management is providing through the dividend payments. The Kalman filter is a well known recursive procedure for computing an estimate of the state of a linear dynamic system subject to noisy and incomplete observation. For a review, see Harvey (1989, Ch.3).

Let us assume that the underlying situation of the firm at time t may be described by means of a *state variable*, indicated as α_t. From the probabilistic point of view, $\{\alpha_t\}_{t=1}^{\infty}$ is a stochastic process whose probability distribution is specified below. From the economic point of view, α_t provides general information relevant to the prosperity of the firm. The information may be firm specific (e.g., permanent earnings, investment opportunities, product market share, managerial skills) or may also concern economy wide conditions (e.g., position in the business cycle, exchange rates). High (and positive) values of α_t correspond to high profitability, and vice versa for low (and negative) realizations. The intuition for having a state variable describing firm's prospects is that, when collecting informations on a particular firm, the market tries to weigh up several (maybe contrasting) issues so that, for example, good investment opportunities with inefficient management in place may not be such a good news as the same investment opportunities with effective managers running firm's operations.

We will assume asymmetric information between the managers of the firm and outside investors. In any period t, the managers can observe the realization of α_t while the market cannot. However, the market can make inference from the observable variables to the unobservable state of the firm. Before specifying the probability distribution of α_t and describing the market inference mechanism, let us examine how dividends and observed earnings are affected by the values taken by the state variable. As far dividend policy is concerned, the point of departure is the partial adjustment model of Lintner, 1956. Lintner conducted interviews with 28 carefully selected companies to investigate their thinking on the determination of dividend policy. His description of how dividends are determined can be summarized in four "stylized facts" (see, e,g., Brealey and Myers, 1992, or Allen and Michaely, 1994):

i) Firms have long-run target dividend payout ratios.
ii) Managers focus on the change in the existing rate of dividend payout, not on the amount of newly established payout as such.
iii) Dividend changes follow shifts in long-run, sustainable earnings. Managers smooth dividends. Transitory earnings changes are unlikely to affect dividend payouts.
iv) Managers are reluctant to make dividend changes that might have to be reversed. They are particularly worried about having to rescind a dividend increase.

Lintner developed a simple model which is consistent with these facts. He suggested that corporate dividend behaviour can be described on the basis of the following equation:

$$\Delta D_t = h_0 + c(D_t^* - D_{t-1}) + u_t \qquad (2.1)$$

where $\Delta D_t = D_t - D_{t-1}$ denotes the changes in dividends, D_t is the actual dividend paid out in time period (year) t, D_t^* is the unobserved target dividend payout, c is the partial adjustment factor (i.e. the speed of adjustment to the difference between the target dividend payout and the last year's payout), h_0 is a constant relating to dividend growth and u_t is an error term assumed to be independently and normally distributed with zero mean. Moreover, the target dividend payout, D_t^*, is assumed to be a fraction γ of the current earnings X_t, i.e.

$$D_t^* = \gamma X_t$$

Thus, Lintner's model is

$$\Delta D_t = h_0 + \gamma c X_t - c D_{t-1} + u_t$$

which we may rewrite as

$$D_t = h_0 + \gamma c X_t + (1 - c)D_{t-1} + u_t \qquad (2.2)$$

With this model and annual data from 1918 through 1941, Lintner was able to explain 85 per cent of the dividends changes in his sample of companies. Fama and Babiak (1968) undertook a more comprehensive study of the Lintner model's performance using data for 392 major industrial firms over the period 1946 through 1964. They also found the Lintner model performed well. Both for its simplicity and for its ability to explain the above mentioned stylized facts, Lintner's model is the starting point of our analysis. However, the introduction of the state variable α_t leads to a slightly modified version of equation (2.2) above. In particular, we assume that the change in dividends is positively associated, through a constant $b > 0$, to the underlying situation of the firm, i.e.

$$D_t = h_0 + \gamma c X_t + (1 - c)D_{t-1} + b\alpha_t + u_t \qquad (2.3)$$

This assumption is tantamount to have the firm following a Lintner's type dividend policy and paying (relatively) higher dividends when the state variable takes high values and (relatively) lower dividends in correspondence to low realizations.

As far as the relation between observable earnings and the value of the (unobservable) state variable, we will assume that at any period t, current earnings X_t are related to the underlying state of the firm through the relation

$$X_t = \beta \alpha_t + w_t \qquad (2.4)$$

where β is a positive constant and w_t is assumed to be normally distributed, with zero mean and variance σ_w^2, and uncorrelated with u_t in all time periods. Again, this assumption implies that high values of α_t are followed on average by subsequent high realized earnings.

Thus, equations (2.3) and (2.4) link the observable variables (dividends and earnings) to the firm's state variable. Up to now we have not yet introduced any assumption concerning the stochastic process which govern the evolution of the α_t. To keep things simple we will assume that the state variable follows a simple stationary AR(1) stochastic process, i.e.

$$\alpha_t = \rho\alpha_{t-1} + \eta_t, \qquad , \qquad 0 \le \rho < 1 \qquad (2.5)$$

where η_t is assumed to be normally distributed with zero mean and variance σ_η^2. This assumption greatly simplifies the analysis that follows and implies some degree of persistency in firm's fortune. For example, we can now simply interpret equation (2.4) by saying that earnings have a persistent component, $\beta\alpha_t$, and a idiosyncratic component, w_t.

Thus, the model we want to investigate is given by equations (2.3)-(2.5). In order to apply the Kalman filter, we need to put the system in the space state form. Rewriting the system of equations (2.3) and (2.4), i.e.

$$D_t = h_0 + \gamma c X_t + (1 - c)D_{t-1} + b\alpha_t + u_t \qquad (2.3)$$
$$X_t = \beta\alpha_t + w_t \qquad (2.4)$$

and substituting in eq.(2.3) the expression for X_t given in eq.(2.4) we get

$$D_t = h_0 + (\gamma c\beta + b)\alpha_t + (1 - c)D_{t-1} + \gamma c w_t + u_t \qquad (2.3)'$$
$$X_t = \beta\alpha_t + w_t \qquad (2.4)'$$

From equations (2.3)' and (2.4)' we see that the 2×1 vector of observable variables $Y_t = (Y_t^{(1)}, Y_t^{(2)})' = (D_t, X_t)'$ is related to the scalar α_t via the following *measurement equation*

$$\begin{pmatrix} D_t \\ X_t \end{pmatrix} = \begin{pmatrix} \gamma c\beta + b \\ \beta \end{pmatrix} \alpha_t + \begin{pmatrix} h_0 + (1 - c)D_{t-1} \\ 0 \end{pmatrix} + \begin{pmatrix} \gamma c w_t + u_t \\ w_t \end{pmatrix}$$
$$(2.6)$$

i.e.

$$Y_t = z\alpha_t + n_t + \epsilon_t \tag{2.6)'}$$

where $z = (\gamma c\beta + b, \beta)'$, $n_t = (n_t^{(1)}, n_t^{(2)})' = (h_0 + (1-c)D_{t-1}, 0)'$
and the vector ϵ_t of disturbances is defined as

$$\epsilon_t = \left(\begin{array}{c} \gamma c w_t + u_t \\ w_t \end{array} \right) \tag{2.7}$$

Given the assumptions on u_t and w_t, the vector ϵ_t has zero mean
and covariance matrix H_t given by

$$var(\epsilon_t) \equiv H = \left(\begin{array}{cc} \gamma^2 c^2 \sigma_w^2 + \sigma_u^2 & \gamma c \sigma_w^2 \\ \gamma c \sigma_w^2 & \sigma_w^2 \end{array} \right) \tag{2.8}$$

As already mentioned, the scalar α_t is not observable from the
market but it is known to be generated by the first-order Markov
process given by eq. (2.3), the *transition equation*. The model
we want to investigate has been therefore now put in the state
space form, with transition and measurement equation given, respectively, by (2.3) and (2.6). The specification of the state space
system is completed by two further assumptions:

 i) the initial state α_0 has mean a_0 and variance q_0;
 ii) the disturbances ϵ_t and η_t are uncorrelated with each other
    in all time periods, and uncorrelated with the initial state.

As the market cannot observe directly the value of the state
variable α_t, it makes an inference from observed current earnings
and dividends to current *prosperity* of the firm, and uses this inferred value of α_t to predict future earnings. We now analyze
how the Kalman filter can be used to model this inference procedure. The derivation of the Kalman filter below rests on the
assumptions that the disturbances and the initial state are normally distributed, A standard result on the multivariate normal
distribution then implies that we can calculate recursively the
distribution of α_t, conditional on the information set at time t.
Since these conditional distributions are themselves normal, they
are completely specified by their means and variances. It is these

quantities which the Kalman filter computes [10]. Let a_{t-1} denote the optimal estimator of α_{t-1} based on the observations up to and including Y_{t-1} and q_{t-1} denote the covariance of the estimation error, i.e.

$$q_{t-1} = E[(\alpha_{t-1} - a_{t-1})^2] \tag{2.9}$$

Given a_{t-1} and q_{t-1}, the optimal estimator of α_t is given by

$$a_{t|t-1} = \rho a_{t-1} \tag{2.10}$$

whilst the covariance of the estimation error is

$$q_{t|t-1} = \rho^2 q_{t-1} + \sigma_\eta^2 \tag{2.11}$$

Equations (2.10) and (2.11) are known as the *prediction equations*. Once the new observation, Y_t, becomes available, the estimation of α_t, $a_{t|t-1}$, can be updated. The *updating equations* are

$$a_t = a_{t|t-1} + q_{t|t-1} z' F_t^{-1} (Y_t - z a_{t|t-1} - n_t) \tag{2.12}$$

and

$$q_t = q_{t|t-1} - (q_{t|t-1})^2 z' F_t^{-1} z \tag{2.13}$$

where

$$F_t = q_{t|t-1} z z' + H \tag{2.14}$$

and the inverse of F_t exists because

$$|F_t| = q_{t|t-1}(b^2 \sigma_w^2 + \beta^2 \sigma_u^2) + \sigma_w^2 \sigma_u^2 > 0$$

In order to interpret the above equations, consider first the conditional mean of Y_t at time $t-1$, namely

$$E_{t-1}(Y_t) \equiv \tilde{Y}_{t|t-1} = z a_{t|t-1} + n_t \tag{2.15}$$

---

[10] Moreover (see, e.g., Harvey, 1989, or Anderson and Moore, 1979) the mean of the conditional distribution of α_t is an optimal estimator of α_t in the sense that it minimizes the mean square error.

where $E_t \equiv E(\cdot|I_t)$ and I_t is the time t market's information set. *Prediction errors* are then defined as

$$\nu_t \equiv Y_t - \tilde{Y}_{t|t-1} = z(\alpha_t - a_{t|t-1}) + \epsilon_t \qquad (2.16)$$

They are also known as *innovations* since they represent the new information in the latest observation. As can be seen from (2.12) they play a key role in updating the estimator of the state variable. The further ν_t is from a null vector, the greater the correction in the estimator of α_t.

Equations (2.12) and (2.13) can also be written as a recursion going directly from a_{t-1} and q_{t-1} to a_t and q_t. We obtain

$$a_t = \rho a_{t-1} + (\rho^2 q_{t-1} + \sigma_\eta^2) z' F_t^{-1} \nu_t \qquad (2.17)$$

and

$$q_t = (\rho^2 q_{t-1} + \sigma_\eta^2) - (\rho^2 q_{t-1} + \sigma_\eta^2)^2 z' F_t^{-1} z \qquad (2.18)$$

The intuition behind the filtering equation (2.17) can now be simply grasped. The first term on the right-hand side gives the expectation based on the previous information. The second term gives the update in expectation based on new information from surprises in dividends and earnings.

Let now to simplify notation

$$k \equiv b^2 \sigma_w^2 + \beta^2 \sigma_u^2 .$$

After some simple algebra, (2.12) and (2.13) reduce to

$$a_t = \frac{\sigma_u^2 \sigma_w^2 a_{t|t-1} + q_{t|t-1} \left[b\sigma_w^2 \left(Y_t^{(1)} - n_t^{(1)}\right) + Y_t^{(2)} \left(\beta\sigma_u^2 - b\gamma c\sigma_w^2\right)\right]}{kq_{t|t-1} + \sigma_u^2 \sigma_w^2}$$

$$(2.19)$$

and

$$q_t = \frac{q_{t|t-1} \sigma_u^2 \sigma_w^2}{kq_{t|t-1} + \sigma_u^2 \sigma_w^2} \qquad (2.20)$$

In terms of precision (i.e. inverse of variance) the last equation reads

$$(q_t)^{-1} = (q_{t|t-1})^{-1} + \frac{k}{\sigma_u^2 \sigma_w^2} \qquad (2.20)'$$

Taken together, (2.10), (2.11), (2.19) and (2.20) make up the Kalman filter. The starting values for the Kalman filter will be specified in terms of a_0 and q_0. Given these initial conditions, the Kalman filter delivers the optimal estimator of the state variable as each new observation becomes available.

Before discussing the issue of prediction some remarks are required to clarify the previous analysis. First of all, the state space model considered so far is *conditionally Gaussian*, in the sense that the disturbances are Gaussian but the system matrices (i.e. the matrices that appear in the measurement and transition equations) are stochastic in that they depend on information, that is observations, available at time $t - 1$. However, they may be regarded as being fixed once we are at time $t - 1$, and the derivation of the Kalman filter goes through exactly as in the standard Gaussian model, with $a_{t|t-1}$ and $q_{t|t-1}$ now interpreted as the mean and the covariance of the distribution of α_t conditional on the information at time $t - 1$. Secondly, note that even if the vector n_t in eq.(2.6)' changes over time, and so strictly speaking the state space model given by equations (2.5) and (2.6) is not time invariant, nonetheless all the properties of time invariant systems in which we are interested can still be applied (see, e.g., Harvey, 1989, p.113). Our analysis is thus substantially simplified. Finally, let us now consider the issue of convergence to a steady state. We say that the Kalman filter has a steady state solution if there exists a time invariant error covariance which satisfies the *Riccati equation*

$$q_{t+1|t} = \frac{\rho^2 q_{t|t-1} \sigma_u^2 \sigma_w^2}{k q_{t|t-1} + \sigma_u^2 \sigma_w^2} + \sigma_\eta^2 \tag{2.21}$$

obtained from equations (2.11) and (2.20). If such a solution exists, we can set

$$q_{t+1|t} = q_{t|t-1} = \bar{q} \tag{2.22}$$

thereby obtaining the *algebraic Riccati equation* (ARE)

$$k\bar{q}^2 + \bar{q}[\sigma_u^2 \sigma_w^2 (1 - \rho^2) - k\sigma_\eta^2] - \sigma_u^2 \sigma_w^2 \sigma_\eta^2 = 0 \tag{2.23}$$

As explained in Harvey (1989, p.118) it is usually difficult to obtain an explicit solution to the ARE (and unfortunately eq.(2.23) is not an exception). However, since the model we are investigating is stable (because $0 \leq \rho < 1$) and the disturbances are normally distributed, we can conclude (see Anderson and Moore, 1979, Section 4.4) that, if $q_{1|0} \geq 0$, then

$$\lim_{t \to \infty} q_{t+1|t} = \bar{q} \tag{2.24}$$

with $\bar{q}$ independent of $q_{1|0}$ and so $q_{t+1|t}$ converges to a steady state.

Now, let us consider the issue of (multistep) prediction. When all T observations have been processed, the filter yields a_T, the optimal estimator of the current state variable and $a_{T+1|T} = \rho a_T$, the state variable in the next time period, based on the full information set. This estimator contains all the information needed to make optimal predictions of the future values of both the state and the observations. More precisely, the multistep prediction equations are given by

$$a_{T+l|T} = \rho a_{T+l-1|T} \tag{2.25}$$

and

$$q_{T+l|T} = \rho^2 q_{T+l-1|T} + \sigma_\eta^2 \tag{2.26}$$

From (2.25) we get

$$a_{T+l|T} = \rho^l a_T \tag{2.27}$$

Taking conditional expectations in the measurement equation at time $T + l$ gives

$$E_T(Y_{T+l}) = z a_{T+l|T} + n_{T+l} \tag{2.28}$$

In particular, we have

$$E_T(X_{T+l}) = \beta a_{T+l|T} = \beta \rho^l a_T \tag{2.29}$$

Now, the market value of the firm is given by

$$V_t = \sum_{l=1}^{+\infty} \frac{E_t(X_{t+l})}{(1+r)^l} - B_t \tag{2.30}$$

where r is the (fixed) interest rate and B_t is the period t level of borrowings. Using (2.29), eq.(2.30) becomes now (for $t = T$)

$$V_T = \beta a_T \sum_{l=1}^{\infty} (\frac{\rho}{1+r})^l - B_T \qquad (2.31)$$

i.e., since $\rho < 1 + r$,

$$V_T = (\frac{\beta\rho}{1+r-\rho}) a_T - B_T \qquad (2.32)$$

Chapter 3

The Effect of Publicly Available Information

3.1 Public Information

We now examine how the market inference procedure is affected by the large amount of publicly available information. In the previous Chapter the process of signal extraction from dividends has been studied in a very simplified framework assuming that no information was available to the market except dividends and earnings. This description of the interaction between firms and shareholders is clearly unrealistic since in fact almost every firm is subject to close market's scrutiny and a large amount of information is produced by financial analysts to help investors to select the best stocks.

In what follows we will model public information as a noisy observation of the unobservable state variable. More precisely, the public signal is assumed to be

$$s_t = \alpha_t + \zeta_t \tag{3.1}$$

where ζ_t has normal distribution with mean zero and precision $\Delta > 0$, and is independent of all other exogenous random variables in the model. If we think of this information as voluntarily disclosed by the firm, then this is tantamount to assuming that the firm is able to precommit to releasing public information of a given precision (as in Diamond, 1985). We assume that disclosure is noisy due to the higher costs of a non noisy disclosure. Even if in principle the firm could observe precisely the value of the state variable, this could be extremely costly, e.g. the cost of the observation can be an increasing unbounded above function of the

precision. This high cost can therefore suggest approximate observation and disclosure. Alternatively, the release of proprietary
information can provide strategic information to potential competitors and this, again, can be extremely costly for the disclosing
firm [11] (see Darrough and Stoughton, 1990). Finally, note that
the above mentioned costs are costs of producing and disseminating the information. But the costs of disclosure are twofold, since
there are also the traders' costs of assimilating the information.
For example, while it is not very costly to obtain a firm's financial
statement (once produced), it is quite costly to understand the
implications of its content [12].

We will now extend the Kalman filter analysis of the previous
Chapter taking into account the new available information given
by eq.(3.1). Correspondigly we will make use of the same notations as before with a superscript Δ added (e.g. a_t, q_t,.. become
a_t^Δ, q_t^Δ,..). As in Chapter 2, we will assume that not only the
disturbances but also the initial state is normally distributed (i.e.
α_0 has a normal distribution with mean $a_0^\Delta = a_0$ and covariance
$q_0^\Delta = q_0$). Moreover, the disturbances are distributed independently (of each other and) of α_0. In order to describe the time
sequence of events let a_{t-1}^Δ denote the optimal estimator of α_{t-1}
based upon both the observations and the information released
up to and including time $t - 1$. At the beginning of period t
each trader's prior beliefs are that α_t has a (conditional) normal
distribution with mean $a_{t|t-1}^\Delta$ and variance $q_{t|t-1}^\Delta$ given by

$$a_{t|t-1}^\Delta = \rho a_{t-1}^\Delta$$

---

[11] In fact almost any information voluntarily revealed through formal
and informal channels (e.g. financial statements or press conferences)
can have strategic implications and can reveal useful information to
competitors. For a discussion of the relationship between disclosure
and competition see Verrecchia, 1990.

[12] The distinction between producing and assimilating information
is made by Merton (1987a) and Fishman and Hagerty (1989). The
latter examine also how taking traders' costs of learning the information
content of firms' disclosures into account can affect incentives to expend
resources on disclosure.

and

$$q_{t|t-1}^{\Delta} = \rho^2 q_{t-1}^{\Delta} + \sigma_{\eta}^2$$

i.e. equations (2.10) and (2.11), respectively, with the Δs added. Public information, s_t, increases the conditional precision of α_t by Δ: normal distribution theory (see Degroot, 1970, p. 54) implies that the traders' conditional precision is now $(q_{t|t-1}^{\Delta})^{-1} + \Delta$, i.e. the variance of the conditional distribution is now

$$q_{t|t-1}^{+} = \frac{q_{t|t-1}^{\Delta}}{1 + q_{t|t-1}^{\Delta}\Delta} \tag{3.2}$$

The signal s_t also makes the conditional mean of α_t vary: it becomes

$$a_{t|t-1}^{+} = a_{t|t-1}^{\Delta} + \frac{\Delta}{q_{t|t-1}^{\Delta} + \Delta}(s_t - a_{t|t-1}^{\Delta}) = \frac{a_{t|t-1}^{\Delta} q_{t|t-1}^{\Delta} + s_t \Delta}{\Delta + q_{t|t-1}^{\Delta}} \tag{3.3}$$

We can now apply the Kalman filter anlysis developed in the previous Chapter. To simplify notation, let

$$k' \equiv b^2 \sigma_w^2 + \beta^2 \sigma_u^2 + \sigma_u^2 \sigma_w^2 \Delta .$$

When the new measurement Y_t (dividends and earnings, see equation (2.6)) is available, the updating equations become (see eqs. (2.19) and (2.20))

$$a_t^{\Delta} = \frac{1}{k' q_{t|t-1}^{\Delta} + \sigma_u^2 \sigma_w^2}\left\{ \sigma_u^2 \sigma_w^2 \frac{a_{t|t-1}^{\Delta} q_{t|t-1}^{\Delta} + s_t \Delta}{q_{t|t-1}^{\Delta} + \Delta} \right.$$

$$\left. + \frac{q_{t|t-1}^{\Delta}}{q_{t|t-1}^{\Delta}\Delta + 1}[b\sigma_w^2 (Y_t^{(1)} - n_t^{(1)}) + Y_t^{(2)}(\beta\sigma_u^2 - b\gamma c\sigma_w^2)] \right\} \tag{3.4}$$

and

$$q_t^{\Delta} = \frac{q_{t|t-1}^{\Delta} \sigma_u^2 \sigma_w^2}{k' q_{t|t-1}^{\Delta} + \sigma_u^2 \sigma_w^2} \tag{3.5}$$

In terms of precision the last equation reads

$$(q_t^{\Delta})^{-1} = (q_{t|t-1}^{\Delta})^{-1} + \frac{b^2 \sigma_w^2 + \beta^2 \sigma_u^2}{\sigma_u^2 \sigma_w^2} + \Delta \qquad (3.5)'$$

In each period t, the described sequence of events may be summarized as follows:

i) The market's prior of α_t is normal with mean $a_{t|t-1}^{\Delta}$ and variance $q_{t|t-1}^{\Delta}$;

ii) Public information is released of the form given in eq.(3.1) ;

iii) A first updating of the prior gives $a_{t|t-1}^{+}$ and $q_{t|t-1}^{+}$;

iv) Earnings and dividends figures are announced ;

v) The final updating gives a_t^{Δ} and q_t^{Δ} ;

vi) On the basis of a_t^{Δ} and q_t^{Δ} the state forecast $a_{t+1|t}^{\Delta}$ and the state forecast error covariance $q_{t+1|t}^{\Delta}$ are evaluated.

Notice that the already established convergence of the sequence $\{q_{t+1|t}\}$ (see Chapter 2) implies the convergence of the $\{q_{t+1|t}^{\Delta}\}$, where

$$q_{t+1|t}^{\Delta} = \frac{\rho^2 q_{t|t-1}^{\Delta} \sigma_u^2 \sigma_w^2}{k' q_{t|t-1}^{\Delta} + \sigma_u^2 \sigma_w^2} + \sigma_\eta^2 ; \qquad (3.6)$$

this is because the recursive structures of the two sequences are exactly the same once we substitute the constant $k = b^2 \sigma_w^2 + \beta^2 \sigma_w^2$ in eq.(2.19) with $k' = k + \sigma_u^2 \sigma_w^2 \Delta$ in eq.(3.6). Obviously the limit will be different, but since for any $\Delta > 0$ we have

$$q_{t+1|t}^{\Delta} < q_{t+1|t} \qquad \forall t$$

it follows that

$$\lim_{t \to \infty} q_{t+1|t}^{\Delta} \leq \lim_{t \to \infty} q_{t+1|t} \qquad \forall \Delta > 0$$

Figures 1 and 2, page 36, explore the dynamics of $q_{t|t-1}^{\Delta}$ (the variances) and $(q_t^{\Delta})^{-1}$ (the precisions) respectively, for different values of the precision Δ in correspondence of the following set of values for the parameters:

$$b = 1.0 \qquad \beta = 20 \qquad \rho = 0.95$$

and

$$\sigma_u^2 = 0.04 \qquad \sigma_w^2 = 4 \qquad \sigma_\eta^2 = 0.0025$$

The initial values are $q_0^\Delta = 0$ and $(q_0^\Delta)^{-1} = 10^{10}$. Notice that for $\Delta = 0$ we have the standard Kalman filter.

We now compare the equations just derived with the analogous expressions obtained in the previous Chapter. First of all notice that when $\Delta = 0$ (i.e. when no effective information is released at any date) then

$$q_{t|t-1}^+ = q_{t|t-1}^\Delta$$

and

$$a_{t|t-1}^+ = a_{t|t-1}^\Delta$$

and so equations (3.4) and (3.5) reduce to (2.12) and (2.13). On the other hand, when $\Delta > 0$, for each t

$$q_{t|t-1}^+ < q_{t|t-1}^\Delta$$

and so, as expected, the public information reduces the market's uncertainty on α_t. Let us now consider how Δ affects the informational content of dividends, i.e. how the information voluntarily released by the firm reduces the amount of information inferred through the dividend figures. To this aim we introduce the function

$$F_t(\Delta) = q_{t|t-1}^+ - q_t^\Delta \tag{3.7}$$

For any given (and fixed) period t, $F_t(\Delta)$ is indicative of the reduction in the market's uncertainty subsequent to a dividend announcement. It is easy to see that, $\forall \Delta > 0$, $F_t(\Delta) > 0$ and $F_t'(\Delta) < 0$, so that $F_t(\Delta)$ is a positive strictly decreasing function of Δ with

$$F_t(0) > 0$$

and

$$\lim_{\Delta \to +\infty} F_t(\Delta) = 0^+$$

The above analysis shows that in any period t the information content of dividends decreases with the amount of information (as measured by Δ) available in the market. Figure 3, page 37, shows the values of $F_t(\Delta)$ for $t = 8$ and in correspondence of the above used values for the parameters.

3.2 Conclusion

This Part of the book has investigated the information contents of dividends in a dynamic setting with learning. The asymmetry of information between the managers of a publicly traded firm and the outsiders investors has been modelled by means of a state variable representing the underlying situation of the firm. The market cannot observe directly the value of the state variable but it can make inference about the state variable from observed dividends and earnings. Furthermore, the market also receives a large amount of public information (some of which is voluntarily disclosed by the firm) which affects this inference mechanism.

The model predicts that the information contained in dividend announcements, as measured by the reduction in the market's uncertainty on the true state of the firm, depends crucially on the amount of information already disseminated in the market. In other words, large amounts of information enable the market to better estimate the firm's state variable and therefore reduces the unexpected part of the dividend change [13].

The results of the model seem to be in accordance with some empirical evidence (as reported by, e.g., Woolridge and Ghosh, 1986) that dividend announcements (especially dividend reductions) by companies subject to scarce market's scrutiny (e.g. sma-

---

[13] For an introduction to the *dividend optical illusion* (i.e. when dividends appear to matter even when they do not) and for an interesting discussion of the role of a Rational Expectations argument on the effects of the management's dividend decisions on the value of the firm, see Miller, 1986.

ller companies) convey more information and have greater surprise value [14].

The model developed in this Part of the book can be extended in several directions. Firstly, the cost for both disseminating and assimilating information are not explicitly incorporated in the model. Moreover, if the public signal is interpreted as information voluntarily disclosed by the firm, then it would be interesting to optimally determine the precision of the information released (once costs are taken into account) as the solution of the managers' optimization problem. This in turn would require to specify the managers' objective function and to solve an optimal control problem [15].

---

[14] See also Eddy and Seifert (1988) for confirmatory evidence of this.

[15] Dreze, 1985, analyzes the problem of defining an appropriate objective function for a firm under conditions of asymmetric information between the insiders and the outsiders.

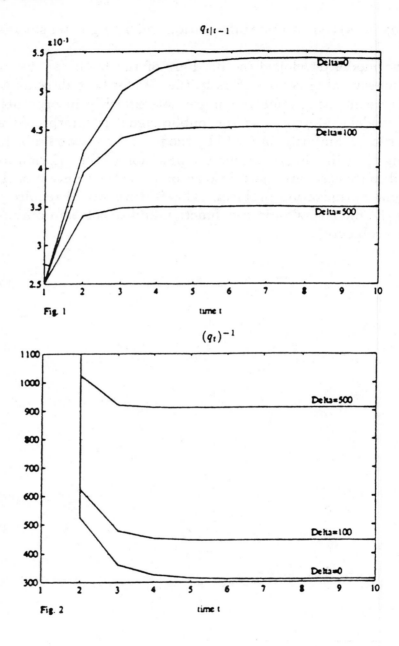

Fig. 1

Fig. 2

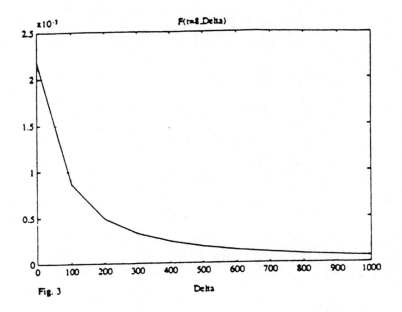

Fig. 3

Part II

Managers and Stock Price

Part II

Draughts and Block Games

Chapter 4

Dividend Policy and Stock Price Volatility

4.1 Introduction

The idea that speculative prices fully and correctly reflect available information is central to modern financial economic theory. However, there is growing evidence that the capital markets may not be informationally efficient and a significant strand of research in the financial economics literature suggests that changes in speculative prices are too volatile to be accounted for by changes in information on economic fundamentals alone. Figure 1, page 64, (from A. Kleidon, 1986a) plots the real value of the Standard and Poor's annual composite index of the U.S. stock market over the past century alongside the ex post realized present value of future dividends [16]. Plots like these [17] show clearly that the stock market has exhibited large fluctuations relative to the baseline of the ex post perfect foresight value. Indeed, at times the real *S&P* stock market index has been more than twice and at times less than half of what its smoothly-growing ex post perfect fore-

---

[16] The $S\&P's$ composite index is taken from Standard and Poor's Securities Price Index and from Cowles et al. (1939). The data series from 1871 to the late 1980s is printed in Shiller (1989). Stock prices are real values for January. Dividends are total for the year divided by the year's average producer price level. In calculating perfect foresight fundamentals, the present value of post-sample dividends is assumed to be equal to the terminal price.

[17] Figure 2, page 65, from Bulkley and Tonks (1989), is a plot similar to Fig.1 (but for detrended prices) for the de Zoete and Wedd annual Equity Price Index in the U.K. Stock Market.

sight value turned out to be. Similar considerations hold for the U.K. Stock Market. Shiller (1981) and LeRoy and Porter (1981) argued that such high volatility relative to perfect foresight fundamental posed severe difficulties for the Efficient Market Hypothesis (EMH). The point here is that a good forecast has to be less variable than, or at most as variable as, the quantity forecasted. Consequently, plots like Figures 1 and 2 seem to contradict the assumption that the current price is a good forecast of the perfect foresight fundamental. Thus, this excess volatility of the market appeared to be strong evidence against the EMH.

4.1.1 Dividends and Prices

In this and in the next two Chapters we investigate the relationship between dividend policy and stock prices in an efficient market. We shift the attention from dividends to earnings and we take the innovation in the present discounted value of earnings as the exogenous source of uncertainty. We show how fairly general assumptions on this innovation process can be used to describe a wide range of dividend processes. This approach allows a great deal of generality for the specific results we derive and is in complete accordance with the recent empirical findings of De Angelo, De Angelo and Skinnert (1994) which conclude their paper on dividend policy and earnings growth with the suggestion that

> " *researchers should more closely study the influence of earnings growth on asset values and corporate financial policies - issues emphasized over thirty years ago by Miller and Modigliani (1961)*"

It has been sometimes argued (see, e.g., Grossman and Shiller, 1981) that the variability of stock prices cannot be accounted for by information regarding future dividends *since dividends just do not seem to vary enough to justify the price movement*. Apart from any empirical regularities of real data, the basic theoretical argument of this frequently told story, i.e. in an efficient market prices cannot fluctuate too much if dividends don't, is wrong. We show this only assuming variance stationarity of prices and dividends. For any given value of the uncertainty about future earnings, we determine regions of trade-off between volatility in dividends and volatility in prices.

4.1.2 Price Volatility

We also develop a new framework to analyze the excess volatility of stock prices. The main attraction of Shiller's work was its model free property, i.e. the variance bounds inequality did not depend on a particular specification of the model for dividends. On the other hand, as the substantial counter literature which followed Shiller's paper has now clearly pointed out, the properties of any econometric test of that inequality can only be investigated conditional on a particular dividends model. In the above described setting, without assuming a priori any specific dividend model and with the innovation in the present discounted value of earnings as the unique source of uncertainty, we are able to fully characterize the conditions leading to violations of the variance bounds inequality. In particular, violations are always associated with extremely smooth dividend policy, in accordance with well known empirical findings. Also, for any given sample length, any investors' forecast horizon and any number of lags affecting the present, we show how it is always possible to obtain violations, i.e. for a suitable choice of the parameters of the model we can always select an appropriate dividend policy such that rational prices violate the variance bounds inequality. Furthermore, the violations will be stronger the shorter the sample length and the investors' forecast horizon and the larger the number of lags affecting the present. We also use numerical simulations to show that the economy in our model can easily reproduce plots similar to those used by Shiller to claim the failure of the efficient market hypothesis, even when prices and dividends are stationary.

4.1.3 Overview of Part II

This Part of the book is organized as follows: in section 4.2 some of the extensive empirical and theoretical literature on excess volatility of stock prices is reviewed. The suggested explanations for excess volatility are presented and critically assessed in section 4.3. Chapter 5 describes the fundamental trade-off between volatility of prices and volatility of dividends in a rational market. Section 6.1 is devoted to the derivation of a general theoretical framework for the variance bounds inequality. The properties of this inequality are investigated further analytically and by means of numerical simulations in section 6.2, where the concept of grossness of a violation is introduced. Conclusions are provided in §6.3.

4.2 The Excess Volatility Debate

Summarizing the major findings of his analysis of stock price volatility over the past century, Robert Shiller concludes his 1981 seminal paper (reprinted as Chapter 5 in Shiller, 1989) by stating that (p.434):

> *"measures of stock price volatility over the past century appear to be far too high - five to thirteen times too high - to be attributed to new information about future real dividends if uncertainty about future dividends is measured by the sample standard deviation of real dividends around their long-run exponential growth path. [..] The failure of the efficient markets model is thus so dramatic that it would seem impossible to attribute the failure to such things as data errors, price index problems, or changes in tax laws."*

These were strong statements and it is not difficult to realize in full the significance of such a conclusion[18]. In this section we

---

[18] Notice, in contrast, that LeRoy and Porter (1981) were much more cautious in commenting their similar findings. They simply presented their evidence as anomalies requiring explanation.

analyze Shiller's original results and we evaluate the soundness of his conclusion in the light of the work offered in its support. After briefly reviewing the basics of market's efficiency, we introduce the variance bounds debate and present the issues that are the bulk of the debate on the alleged excess volatility of stock prices.

4.2.1 - The Variance Bounds Inequlity

There is no universally accepted definition of the term efficient or rational markets theory. The most frequently cited version of this theory is the one presented by Fama (1976, Chapter 5) which is a revision, with some corrections, of his original treatment (Fama, 1970) [19]. According to Fama, the efficient market theory states that asset prices fully reflect all the available information. A capital market is efficient when a) it does not neglect any information relevant to the determination of securities prices and b) it has rational expectations. The assumption of rational expectations means that investors use their informations to make those inferences about future events which are justified by the objective correlations between the information variables and future events, and only those inferences. In other words, in forming expectations about next period's price or rate of return, the market uses the correct probability distributions and all available information. Fama emphasized that efficiency can be tested only jointly with some particular model of market equilibrium, the nature of which depend on endowments and preferences but which is not implied by market efficiency.

As far as the interpretation of the available empirical evidence is concerned, in his 1970 paper Fama concluded that the evidence strongly but non unanimously supported market efficiency. However, towards the end of the Seventies, a series of papers by Robert Shiller (1979, 1981) and Stephen LeRoy and Richard Porter (1981) put into question the efficiency of the markets. From their analysis, largely based upon the variance bounds inequality, asset prices appeared to be far more volatile than is consistent with the efficient markets model. The variance bounds inequality can be eas-

---

[19] For a more recent review of market efficiency, see Fama, 1991.

ily derived in the constant expected return model. In an efficient market all available information is fully reflected in the price of a security: if we further assume that the discount rate is time invariant, then the stock price at the beginning of time t, p_t, can be written as

$$p_t = \frac{E(p_{t+1} + d_{t+1} | I_t)}{1 + r} \tag{4.1}$$

where d_t is the dividend and r is the constant real expected return. $E(\cdot | I_t)$ is mathematical expectation conditional on the market's period-t information set I_t. (When there is no ambiguity about the information set, as here, we will simply write E_t for $E(\cdot | I_t)$). Assume now that agent never forgets the past, so that I_{t+1} is more informative than I_t, and therefore the rule of iterated expectations guarantees, e.g., that $E_t[E_{t+1}(p_{t+2})] = E_t(p_{t+2})$ and similarly for dividends. Substituting recursively for p_{t+1}, p_{t+2} etc, from (4.1) we have

$$p_t = E_t \Big[\sum_{k=1}^{n} \frac{d_{t+k}}{(1+r)^k} + \frac{p_{t+n}}{(1+r)^n} \Big] \tag{4.2}$$

Suppose that the terminal condition

$$\lim_{n \to \infty} E_t \Big(\frac{p_{t+n}}{(1+r)^n} \Big) = 0 \tag{4.3}$$

holds (to rule out speculative bubbles). Then (4.2) implies that

$$p_t = E_t \Big[\sum_{k=1}^{\infty} \frac{d_{t+k}}{(1+r)^k} \Big] \tag{4.4}$$

i.e. stock prices are equal to the expected present value of future dividends. At this stage it is worth noticing, for its relevance in empirical analysis, that the expected present value model (4.4) implies that rates of return on stock are a fair game [20] and the

---

[20] A stochastic process x_t is a *martingale* with respect to a sequences of information sets I_t if x_t has the property that

$$E(x_{t+1} | I_t) = x_t$$

reverse implication also obtains: indeed , we could have alternatively derived the model (4.4) from the fair game assumption for rates of return on stock, defined as the sum of the dividend yield plus capital gain less one (see LeRoy, 1989, for details).

Define now a new variable, p_t^*, as

$$p_t^* = \sum_{k=1}^{\infty} \frac{d_{t+k}}{(1+r)^k} \tag{4.5}$$

Being the present value of actual subsequent values of d_t, this variable is called *the perfect foresight* or *ex post rational price* in much of the variance bounds literature. A comparison of (4.4) and (4.5) shows that

$$p_t = E_t(p_t^*) \tag{4.6}$$

This implies that

$$p_t^* = p_t + u_t \tag{4.7}$$

where u_t is the forecast error which, by virtue of p_t being an optimal forecast of p_t^*, will be uncorrelated with p_t, so that $cov(u_t, p_t)$ will be zero. From (4.7) it follows that $var(p_t) + var(u_t) = var(p_t^*)$ and since variances are non negative we therefore obtain the variance bounds [21]

$$var(p_t) \leq var(p_t^*) \tag{4.8}$$

However, when the inequality is tested empirically using sample variances of prices and p_t^* under the assumption of stationary and ergodic processes for prices and dividends, it appears to be grossly

---

where it is assumed that x_t is in I_t. A stochastic process y_t is a *fair game* if it has the property

$$E(y_{t+1} | I_t) = 0.$$

It is obvious that x_t is a martingale if and only if $x_{t+1} - x_t$ is a fair game (and for this reason fair games are also called *martingale differences*).

[21] Shiller (1981) derived two further inequalities involving first differences of prices and dividends. Because most attention has been focused on (4.8), we will concentrate on the first variance bounds (4.8).

violated. Shiller implementation of an operational test of the inequality (4.8) was simple and direct. To correct for trend, he divided the variables p_t and p_t^* by a simple growth trend $\lambda^t = e^{bt}$. The parameter b was estimated over the entire sample by regressing log price on time and a constant [22]. To solve the problem that p_t^* is not observable without error, since the summation in (4.5) extends to infinity, Shiller suggested choosing an arbitrary value of p_t^* based on the observed sample $\{p_t\}_{t=1}^T$, for example setting $p_T^* = p_T$ or $p_T^* = p^*(T)$, where

$$p^*(T) = \frac{1}{T} \sum_{t=1}^{T} p_t \tag{4.9}$$

and T is the number of years in the sample period; p_t^* can then be determined recursively by

$$p_t^* = \frac{p_{t+1}^* + d_{t+1}}{1 + r} \tag{4.10}$$

working backwards from T. Given a computed ex post rational series, sample estimates of the various variances (or standard deviations, as has usually been the case) can be calculated and the inequality examined. The result was a striking violation of the bound: as summarized by Shiller in the paragraph cited at the outset of this section, the results reported in his Table 2 (1981, p.431) show that the variance bound in (4.7) is grossly violated by both his *S&P* 1871-1979 data set and his modified Dow Industrial 1928-79 data set. For example, the ratio of sample standard deviation of price to the sample standard deviation of p_t^* for *S&P* data (1871-1979) is 5.59. There are, however, a number of problems with the Shiller's approach, and these form the basis of the Flavin (1983), Kleidon (1986a, 1986b) and Marsh and Merton

---

[22] Shiller used this detrending procedure in his original 1981 paper: because the detrended price for time t depended on information not available at time t, many people thought that perhaps the apparent excess volatility had to do with a spurious estimated trend, or a spurious estimated constant term, or both (see Shiller, 1989, for further details.)

(1986, 1987) critiques of such volatility tests. These econometric issues are discussed in turn in the following subsections.

4.2.2 Small Sample Bias

Much of the impact of the variance bounds literature has come from the apparent clear violation of the inequality (4.8) by plots such as figure 1. Indeed, while the inequality seems to imply that the time series plot of p_t should be smoother than that of p_t^*, the actual plots of p_t and p_t^* are striking evidence against this implication [23]. However, the drawing of such an implication would be unwarranted since the greater smoothness of the p_t^* series is the basic result underlying the effect of the small sample bias in stock price variance bounds tests. Before examining in details this effect, a preliminary remark is in order. As Kleidon (1986a) pointed out, the inequality (4.8) is essentially a cross-section relation across different economies; figures 1 and 2 give instead time series plots for a single economy. In other words, the bound (4.8) is derived with respect to value of p_t^* that differ from each other at date t because different realizations of future dividends have different present values at date t. These different realizations occur across the different economies or worlds that may possibly occur in the future, looking forward from date t. Using a geometric random walk model for dividends, Kleidon is able to reproduce, by simulation, plots that look very similar to figures 1 and 2 but where prices are set rationally by (4.4) (see Kleidon, 1986a, fig. 2 p.956). The conclusion is that tests of the bound (4.8) using time series data from only one economy, require additional strong assumptions (as we mentioned before and we will discuss further below, essentially stationarity and ergodicity) beyond those needed to derive (4.8) and care must be exercised to ensure that the "variances" discussed with respect to time series data correspond to those in the variance inequality.

In order to explain how small sample bias has been affecting the original results of asset price excess volatility, we will now

---

[23] Such plots often seemed so convincing that they substituted for formal statistical evidence (see, e.g., Tirole, 1985, p. 1085).

examine what should be expected in plots of time series of price and p_t^* for a single economy. A classical example (Kleidon, 1986a and 1986b and Gilles and LeRoy, 1991) will facilitate the understanding of the issues at stake and will aid in the exposition of the sampling problems that attend the empirical implementation of tests of the variance bounds inequality. Assume for dividends a stationary AR(1) process, i.e.

$$d_t = \mu_d + \rho d_{t-1} + \epsilon_t \tag{4.11}$$

where μ_d is a constant, $|\rho| < 1$ and ϵ_t is independent and identically distributed (i.i.d.) $(0, \sigma_\epsilon^2)$. Also assume that the information set I_t comprises current and past dividends. Then, under the rational valuation model (4.4), the stochastic process governing the behaviour of actual prices is a stationary AR(1) process with the same autoregressive parameter as dividends, i.e.

$$p_t = \mu_p + \rho p_{t-1} + \delta_t \tag{4.12}$$

where $\mu_p = \mu_d / r$ and $\delta_t = \epsilon_t \rho / (1 + r - \rho)$. Also, given the dividend process (4.11) and assuming $|1/(1 + r)| < 1$, the stochastic process generating perfect foresight prices p_t^* is the stationary AR(2) process given by

$$(1 - \phi_1 B - \phi_2 B^2) p_t^* = \mu_{p^*} + \psi_t \tag{4.13}$$

where

$$\phi_1 = \rho + \left(\frac{1}{1+r}\right)$$

$$\phi_2 = -\rho\left(\frac{1}{1+r}\right)$$

$$\mu_{p^*} = \frac{\mu_d}{1+r}$$

$$\psi_t = \frac{\eta_{t+1}}{1+r}$$

and where $E(\eta_t) = E(\epsilon_t)$, $var(\eta_t) = var(\epsilon_t) = \sigma_\epsilon^2$, and B is the backshift operator. Now, the price processes (4.12) and (4.13) have well defined unconditional variances, namely

$$var(p_t) = \left(\frac{\rho}{1+r-\rho}\right)^2 \frac{\sigma_\epsilon^2}{(1-\rho^2)} \tag{4.14}$$

and (see Box and Jenkins, 1976)

$$var(p_t^*) = \frac{\sigma_\epsilon^2(1+r+\rho)}{(1+r-\rho)(2r+r^2)(1-\rho^2)} \tag{4.15}$$

so that the inequality (4.8) is readily verified as

$$\Delta = var(p_t^*) - var(p_t)$$
$$= \frac{\sigma_\epsilon^2(1+r)^2}{(1+r-\rho)^2(2r+r^2)} > 0$$

for $r > 0$ and $\sigma_\epsilon^2 > 0$.

In order to analyze the characteristics (and, in particular, the property of smoothness) of time series plots of price and p_t^*, let us first notice that (see Kleidon, (1986a), p.961) the same model (4.6) also implies that, for finite k,

$$var(p_t^*|I_{t-k}) \geq var(p_t|I_{t-k}) \quad , \quad k = 0,\ldots\infty \tag{4.16}$$

where $I_{t-k} \subseteq I_t$. The inequality (4.16) is important for several reasons. First, it is clearly useful if conditional variances ($k < \infty$) are defined but unconditional variances ($k = \infty$) are not. For example, in the above described case of prices and dividends following a stationary AR(1) process, the limit as $k \to \infty$ of these conditional variances are the unconditional variances used in (4.8). On the other hand, in the limit case of (nonstationary) random walk, the unconditional variances are not defined , so that inequality (4.8) involves, strictly speaking, undefined terms, although (4.16) can be examined. The last inequality is also important because the smoothness of time series plots of price and p_t^* is also determined by conditional variances, although they differ from those in (4.16) and do not satisfy an inequality such as (4.16). Indeed, it seems reasonable to take the smoothness, or amount of short-term variation in p_t and p_t^*, to be determined by the variance conditional on past values of the series, i.e. $var(p_t|p_{t-k})$ and $var(p_t^*|p_{t-k}^*)$, respectively [24]. We then clearly see that the latter conditional

---

[24] Note that $var(p_t|p_{t-k})$ is equivalent to $var(p_t|I_{t-k})$, once the information set I_t consists of current and past dividends and prices are given by the process (4.12).

variance is not equivalent to $var(p_t^*|I_{t-k})$ since, by the definition of p_t^*, past values of p_t^* depend on future values of d_t, which are not known at or prior to time t. Therefore there is not requirement for $var(p_t|p_{t-k})$ and $var(p_t^*|p_{t-k}^*)$ to satisfy any inequality such as (4.16), and indeed they do not. For example, if dividends follow the stationary AR(1) process (4.11) and the rationally set prices follow the stationary AR(1) process (4.12), then

$$var(p_t|p_{t-k}) = \frac{\sigma_\epsilon^2 \rho^2 (1 - \rho^{2k})}{(1 + r - \rho)^2 (1 - \rho^2)} \qquad (4.17)$$

and, assuming that ϵ_t in (4.11) is normally distributed,

$$var(p_t^*|p_{t-k}^*) = var(p_t^*)(1 - \rho_k^2) \qquad (4.18)$$

where

$$\rho_k = \frac{cov(p_t^*, p_{t-k}^*)}{var(p_t^*)}$$

As shown by Kleidon (1986a and 1986b), for small k,

$$var(p_t|p_{t-k}) > var(p_t^*|p_{t-k}^*) \qquad (4.19)$$

i.e. the inequality (4.16) is reversed and this holds for quite large k, depending on the size of the AR(1) parameter: the closer this parameter is to (but strictly less than) one, the greater the value of k must be before the above inequality is reversed. [25]

The above argument implies that the observed smoothness of p_t^* provides no evidence against the variance bound (4.8) nor against the present value model (4.4). Indeed, as explained above, to test the variance bounds inequality using sample variances of prices and p_t^* requires the additional assumption of stationary and ergodic processes for prices an dividends. However, even when those assumptions are satisfied and so population variances exist and are consistently estimated by sample variances, a small

---

[25] For k large enough, $var(p_t^*|p_{t-k}^*)$ must exceed $var(p_t|p_{t-k})$, since the bound (4.8) holds for unconditional variances.

(or, more correctly, a finite) sample bias results in incorrect apparent rejection of (4.8) in a large proportion of tests based on sample variances. The point here is that estimates of sample variances based on sample means, rather than population means, are downward-biased: this is because the series of p_t^* (and similarly for the p_t) are positively autocorrelated. Furthermore, the bias is considerably more severe for p_t^* (p_t^* is more strongly positively autocorrelated than p_t), so that the test of (4.8) is biased upward, i.e. the inequality is violated far too often. This is established by Kleidon (1986b) [26] for the model in which dividends follow an AR(1) process, with the severity of the bias increasing with the AR(1) parameter. For large (i.e. close to 1) values of the parameter, the point estimates frequently appear to reject the bound even in sample as large as 3,000. However, as reported by Kleidon, the results of the simulations show that the small sample bias, at least by itself, does not seem sufficient to account for the reported gross violations of the bound.

4.2.3 The Issue of Stationarity

As mentioned above, variance bounds tests examine restrictions on the volatility of actual stock price implied by the efficient markets hypothesis. Because stock price appeared to be too volatile to be determined by the expected discounted value of dividends, the hypothesis was rejected by Shiller. However, this conclusion was followed by a great deal of discussion. The strongest criticism against Shiller's claim on the failure of the efficient market theory came from Marsh and Merton (1986). In reassessing Shiller's original findings of excessive volatility, they correctly pointed out that, in formulating his variance bounds test, Shiller makes three basic economic assumptions: (S.1) stock prices reflect investor beliefs, which are rational expectations of future dividends; (S.2) the real expected rate of return on the

---

[26] The same criticism of Shiller's econometric tests is also made by Flavin (1983). She also pointed out that Shiller's (1981) procedure for calculating an observable version of p_t^* also induces bias toward rejection.

stock market is constant over time; (S.3) aggregate real dividends
on the stock market can be described by a finite-variance stationary stochastic process with a deterministic exponential growth
rate. On these premises, Marsh and Merton conclude that, even
if Shiller's results are true rejections, then they reject the joint
hypothesis (S.1), (S.2) and (S.3) which need not, of course, imply
rejection of (S.1). Moreover, to show that the variance bounds
methodology cannot be used to test the hypothesis of stock market rationality, Marsh and Merton develop an alternative variance
bound test. In a model where the dividend is a positive distributed
lag of past stock prices, they show that if observed prices were to
satisfy Shiller variance bound test, then this same sample of prices
would fail their test, and conversely. It would seem, therefore, that
for any set of stock market price data, the hypothesis of market
rationality can be rejected by some variance bound test. This
seeming paradox arises from differences in assumptions about the
underlying stochastic processes used to describe the evolution of
dividends and rational stock prices. Both Shiller and Marsh and
Merton variance bound theorems share in common the hypothesis
(S.1) and (S.2) that stock prices are rationally determined and the
real discount rate is constant. Hence neither (S.1) nor (S.2) of the
respective joint hypothesis is the source of each theorem's con-
tradictory conclusion to the other. It therefore follows necessarily
that the class of aggregate dividend processes postulated by Marsh
and Merton is incompatible with the Shiller theorem assumption
(S.3) of a regular stationary process for detrended aggregate dividends. That is, given that (S.1) and (S.2) hold, nonstationarity
of the dividend process is a necessary condition for the validity of
the Marsh and Merton theorem, whereas stationarity of the dividend process is a sufficient condition for the validity of Shiller's
inequality. Thus, the opposite conclusion of these variance bound
theorems follows directly from the differences in their posited dividend processes.

The issue raised above of the temporal stability of prices and
dividends is central to the debate over the validity of the efficient
market hypothesis. And, indeed, much of the debate which followed the Shiller and LeRoy and Porter papers has focused on the

issue of nonstationarity of the relevant stochastic processes. As pointed out by Merton (1987b), the amount of light that variance bound tests can shed on the issue of market rationality seems to depend critically on the way in which we model the uncertainty surroundings future economic fundamentals. That is, if underlying economic fundamentals are such that the level of rationally determined real and detrended stock prices can be described by a stationary process, then they have power. If, instead, is the percentage change in stock prices that is better described by a stationary process, then they have no power. The resolution of the debate seems therefore to be essentially an empirical matter. Unfortunately, up to now the results have been at a minimum ambiguous. Apart from any econometric flaw in the original Shiller and LeRoy and Porter papers, the point here is whether dividends are trend stationary (as originally supposed by Shiller) or integrated (as assumed by Marsh and Merton). Marsh and Merton, (1987), present empirical evidence in support of the class of aggregate dividend processes they postulate in their variance bound test. On the other hand, in the most thorough study on the issue of the temporal stability of dividends and stock prices, DeJong and Whiteman (1991) tested trend-stationarity against first-difference stationarity of dividends and prices in the US stock market and concluded that these series are more likely to be trend stationary than integrated, thus confirming Shiller's original stationarity assumption and, at the same time, leaving the determination of prices a puzzle.

4.3 Explaining Excess Volatility

In this section, we will briefly review the suggested explanations for excess volatility of asset prices.

4.3.1 Rational Bubbles

As already mentioned, variance bound tests examine restrictions on the volatility of actual stock prices implied by the efficient market hypothesis. Notice that the formal derivation of the variance bounds inequality (4.8) only requires a) the assumption of a constant discount rate and b) the transversality condition (4.3). Before examining the consequences of assuming time-varying real interest rates, it is interesting to consider what happens when (4.3) is not satisfied. Sochastic difference equations such as (4.1) have a multiplicity of solutions. The solution (4.4) is unique provided that the terminal condition (4.3) holds. But if not, there are an infinity of solutions

$$p_t = E_t [\sum_{k=1}^{\infty} \frac{d_{t+k}}{(1+r)^k}] + b_t$$

$$\equiv p_t^f + b_t \qquad (4.20)$$

where b_t is any variable that satisfies $E(b_t | I_{t-1}) = (1+r) b_{t-1}$, i.e. $b_t = (1+r) b_{t-1} + v_t$, with $E(v_t | I_{t-1}) = 0$, and the "f" superscript on p_t^f refers to dependence on fundamentals only. b_t is by definition a rational bubble, an otherwise extraneous event that affects stock prices because everyone expects it to do so. Since the solution (4.20) satisfies the first order condition (4.1), expected return are constant and there are no arbitrage possibilities. [27]. The theory of rational bubbles is an example of a model in which expectations are formed rationally, the market is informationally efficient, but there are large deviations between market prices and fundamental value. Because $(1+r)$ is greater than one for positive values of r, the bubble term is expected to grow and one can construct (see, e.g., Blanchard and Watson, 1982) bubble processes that each period with some probability can experience a large drop, or crash. Rational speculative bubbles allow stock prices to deviate from their fundamental value without assuming irrational investors. Investors realize that prices exceed fundamental values, but they believe that the bubble will continue to grow and to generate high return. The probability of a high return exactly compensates investors for the probability of a crash; therefore, despite the overvaluation, it is perfectly rational to stay in the market.

---

[27] Rational bubbles are also possible with time varying expected returns. The constant expected return model is here used only for simplicity.

4.3.2 Time Varying Discount Rates

As explained above, the model (4.4) and therefore the variance bound that follows from it, requires only the terminal condition (4.3) and a constant expected return. So if there is excess volatility in the population and bubbles are ruled out, the obvious candidate to explain any excess price volatility is movements in expected returns. This was of course among the explanations proposed in some of the first published comments on volatility tests. Unfortunately, if we modify the model (4.4) to allow real discount rates to vary through time, then the model becomes untestable: since we cannot observe directly real discount rates, for any behaviour of prices and dividends, there will always be a discount rate series that makes (4.4) identically satisfied. However, two related questions can be addressed: first, it seems interesting to ask if the required movements in the real discount rate are not larger than we might expect. Second, we would like to know if movements in the current one period discount rate together with new information about such movements in future discount rates can account for high stock price volatility. Both these issues are discussed in Shiller's 1981 paper. As an indicator of real interest rates, Shiller used the four-six-month prime commercial paper rate. This is a nominal interest rate, and therefore its fluctuations should represent both changes in inflationary expectations and interest rate movements. Furthermore, the series of commercial paper rate shows much more fluctuation than one would normally expect in an expected real interest rate. For example, in the sample used by Shiller the commercial paper rate ranges from 0.53% to 9.87%. Nonetheless, while these large movements produce an ex-post rational price series which fluctuate much more than the analogous series evaluated with a constant discount rate, the standard deviation of p_t^* was still found by Shiller to be less than half of the standard deviation of actual prices. Other more recent studies also conclude that the movements in expected return necessary to rationalize stock price movements are too large to be considered reasonable.

4.3.3 Challenges to Rational Expectations

The asset pricing models described in the previous sections are all based on the Rational Expectations Equilibrium conceptualization. Indeed, during the last three decades the Theory of Rational Expectations has been the dominant doctrine employed in the construction of equilibrium models of asset prices and returns. The idea of Rational Expectations has two components: first, that each person's behaviour can be described as the outcome of maximizing an objective function subject to perceived constraints; and, second, that the constraints perceived by everybody in the system are mutually consistent (Sargent, 1993). The first part is a requirement that individual behaviour should be optimal according to some perceived constraints, while the second is a requirement of the consistency of those perceptions across people and with reality. A Rational Expectations Equilibrium is then a fixed point of a mapping from a perceived law of motion for the model's endogenous state variables to an actual law of motion. This notion of equilibrium imputes to the people inside the model much more knowledge about the system they are operating in than is available to the economist who is using the model to try to understand their behaviour [28].

The idea of Rational Expectations clearly provides a logically consistent way for a model builder to close his model. However, is it sensible to expect humans to perform the kind of behaviour which Rational Expectations require them to perform? Moreover, is it sensible to require that the rationality of economic agents be conditioned on their possession of knowledge and skills that none of us possess? In this subsection we will briefly present and compare three recent attempts to explain stock price volatility which share the common characteristics of somehow questioning and to some extent relaxing the assumptions underlying the theory of Rational Expectations. They will be presented following an increasing degree of departure from the standard paradigm. The

---

[28] *"In particular, an econometrician faces the problem of estimating probability distributions and laws of motion that the agents in the model already know."* (Sargent, 1993, page 4)

first allows for learning within the Rational Expectations framework and can therefore be included in the bounded rationality approach. The second is a new approach to the theory of expectations formation in a dynamic context. Finally the third, in sharp contrast with neoclassical doctrine, involves directly irrational behaviour.

As mentioned above (see §4.2), criticism of the excess volatility results has focused on the statistical properties of the original tests performed on time series of price data. However, the precise interpretation of these findings has been questioned by Bulkley and Tonks (1989). The point of departure of their analysis is that before rejecting the Rational Expectations/Efficient Market Hypothesis we need a thorough understanding of which particular interpretation of Rational Expectations is at stake. As is well known, Benjamin Friedman (1979) argued that the assumption that prices are formed as if agents know the true model which generated the data is an extreme assumption about the agents' information set. He therefore suggested to break down the Rational Expectations Hypothesis into two distinct components, namely a behavioural hypothesis, according to which agents use efficiently whatever information is available, and a specific assumption on the available set of information. If the information technology of the economy is such that agents use the true model to generate forecast, then we have Rational Expectations in the strong form. On the other hand, if agents forecast using an estimated model we have Rational Expectations in the weak form. Bulkley and Tonks (1989) argued that conventional variance bound tests in fact test the strong form of the Rational Expectations/Efficient Market Hypothesis. This seems to be too a strong assumption about information. A more reasonable hypothesis is instead to assume that agents form expectations using a model estimated using unbiased techniques. In their study of volatility in the U.K. market, Bulkley and Tonks show that although the conventional variance bound is violated, the bound appropriate to a test of the weak form of the Rational Expectations Hypothesis is satisfied. This suggests that some part of the excess volatility of actual stock prices reported in previous tests can be attributed to revision in the parameters of an agent's estimated model of the dividend process.

The intuition that learning may help to explain the apparent excess volatility of stock prices has been further developed by Timmermann (1993, 1994), who provides an explicit analysis of convergence and stability of learning in the U.K. stock market. Timmermann assumes that agents use recursive estimation to update the parameters of their model and use the estimated model to form expectations. In turn the estimated model will feed back on the actual law of motion of the economy, thus generating a complex dynamic system. Notice that if dividends were following an exogenous time-invariant stochastic process, agents' estimates of the dividend and price equation would eventually converge to their true value. On the other hand, when there is feedback from stock prices to dividends, convergence of the learning procedure is no longer guaranteed and there may in fact be multiple equilibria. The feedback from stock prices to dividends can be explained by companies' use of stock prices as a forward looking indicator that summarizes earnings prospects. Assuming that companies target a dividend-earning payout ratio (as suggested in the classic Lintner 1956 study), it will be optimal for them to condition their dividends on the information which can be inferred from stock prices. Seen in this light, the economic intuition for multiple equilibria in present value models with a feedback from stock prices to dividends is that these equilibria represent different degree of firms' beliefs on how informative stock prices are about future earnings. The main result of Timmemann's analysis is that the convergence of learning crucially depends on the prior information agents impose on the learning process. If agents attempt to learn the long-run dynamics of the model without imposing strong prior information, then their learning cannot converge to a Rational Expectations Equilibrium. If, on the other hand, agents have strong priors and impose a unit root on their model, thus confining their learning to the short-run dynamics of the model, then their recursive learning may converge to a Rational Expectations Equilibrium. However, in this case learning will induce substantial volatility in stock prices on the path to the equilibrium.

A new approach to the theory of expectations formation, developed at Stanford University by Mordecai Kurz (Kurz 1994a, 1994b, 1994c and 1994d), is another recent attempt to explain (among several other things) excess volatility of stock prices challenging the dominant paradigm of the theory of Rational Expectations. This approach studies the formation of expectations in a dynamic context in which ample past data on the performance of the system are available. Furthermore, Kurz postulates that agents base their expectations only on the knowledge of those observable past data, but have no a priori *structural knowledge* (i.e. they do not need to know demand and supply functions, they do not need to be able to compute general equilibrium, etc.). The assumption of structural knowledge is rejected by Kurz not because there is anything logically wrong with it, but because it appears to be empirically flawed: it requires of economic agents to do what no human can do and therefore the identification of rationality with the possession of extraordinary structural knowledge would be hardly justifiable (Kurz, 1994c). In contrast, Kurz proposes to base the rationality of beliefs on a requirement of compatibility of those agents' beliefs with empirical distributions. This leads him to derive a theory of equilibrium with diversity of rational beliefs called rational Beliefs Equilibrium. Kurz (1994d) shows that in a Rational Beliefs Equilibrium agents make rational forecasting mistakes and, furthermore, the aggregate mistakes of the agents induce extra volatility of economic variables above and beyond the level that would be generated by the volatility of exogenous variables. Kurz calls this internally propagated uncertainty *Endogenous Uncertainty*. This analysis is at too early a stage to fully assess its relevance. A more general theoretical framework is required before evaluating the importance of rational mistakes on price fluctuations.

The third recent attempt to explain excess volatility of stock prices challenging the theory of Rational Expectations tries to model explicitly the behaviour of irrational investors. Even if within the paradigm of neoclassical economics rationality is part of the inner core, nonetheless in recent years there has been increasing interest in irrational behaviour as a possible explanation of several financial anomalies. First of all, it is part of the conventional wisdom on Wall Street that financial markets overreact. This view is supported both by casual observation and academic research. For example, Shiller's 1987 survey evidence reveals that investors were reacting to each other during the October crash rather than to hard economic news. A similar conclusion is reached by French and Roll (1986) who find that prices are more volatile when markets are open than when they are closed. DeBondt and Thaler (1985, 1987) argue that mean reversion in stock prices is evidence of overreaction. In their 1985 paper, they show that extreme loser stocks over an initial three to five years period earned excess returns over the subsequent three to five years. In their 1987 paper, they show that these excess returns cannot easily been attributed to changes in risk, tax effects or the "small firm anomaly". Rather they argue that the excess return to losers might be explained by biased expectations of the future, i.e. by excessive pessimism about the future prospects of companies that had done poorly. In other words, psychological and sociological evidence seems to be consistent with individuals following irrational trading rules, overreacting to news (see also Shiller, 1984, for fads in stock prices). Potentially, this both generates wide variations in expected returns and renders inadequate traditional models of return determination.

Another interpretation of fads in stock prices is that while some fraction of trading is done by naive investors, another fraction of trading is done by sophisticated investors. In a series of papers, De Long, Shleifer, Summers and Waldmann study a model of a stock market in which there are both rational traders, who form their price expectations accurately according to fundamentals, and noise traders, who misperceive fundamental values (see De Long, Shleifer, Summers and Waldmann, 1990, 1991). Contrary to the classical thesis of Milton Friedman (1953) that only rational traders stay in the market in the long run, they show that noise traders can survive and even prosper, the reason being that the risk created by the unpredictability of unsophisticated investors' opinions significantly reduces the attractiveness of arbitrage. As long as arbitrageurs have short horizons and so must worry about liquidating their investment in a mispriced asset, their aggressiveness will be limited even in the absence of fundamental risk. In this case noise trading can lead to a large divergence between market prices and fundamental values. Furthermore, because noise trader risk limits the effectiveness of arbitrage, the price of the risky asset (to be intended as aggregated equities) is excessive volatile in the sense that it moves more that can be explained on the basis of changes in fundamental values. Such excess volatility becomes even easier to explain if the assumption that all market participants are either noise traders or sophisticated investors who bet against them is relaxed. A more reasonable assumption seems to be that many traders pursue passive strategies, neither responding to noise nor betting against noise traders. If a large fraction of investors allocate a constant fraction of their wealth to the risky asset (i.e. to equities), then even a small measure of noise traders can have a large impact on prices, since only a few sophisticated investors are willing to hold extra stock when noise traders try to sell. Price must therefore fall considerably for noise investors to sell, and the fewer sophisticated investors there are relative to the noise traders, the larger will be the impact of noise.

While traditional present-value models are well enough specified that one can potentially argue that these models cannot adequately explain stock prices volatility, the same cannot probably be said for models involving irrational investors' behaviour (fads, overreaction, noise traders, etc.). The quantitative evidence in favour of the latter as an explanation of stock price volatility is largely indirect, in the form of negative verdicts on traditional models for returns.

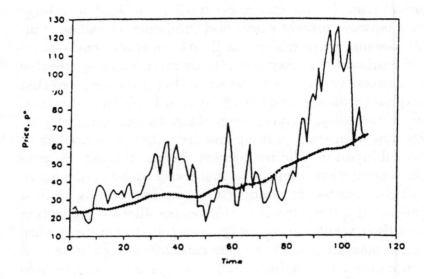

Fig. 1
Standard and Poor's real annual composite stock price index 1926-1979 aug-
mented with Cowles Commission common stock index 1871-1925 (solid line)
and ex-post realized present value of future dividends during the same period.

Source: A. Kleidon (1986a), Variance Bounds Tests and Stock Price Valuation
Models, *Journal of Political Economy*

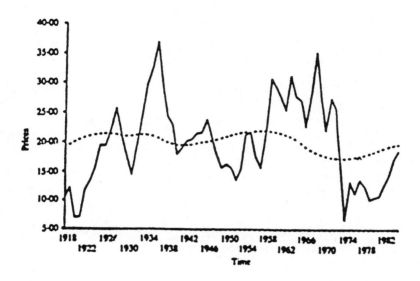

Fig. 2
De Zoete and Wedd annual equity price index in the U.K. stock market (de-trended actual prices: —) and ex-post realized present value of future dividends (detrended ex-post rational prices: ···) 1918-1982.

Source: G. Bulkley and I. Tonks (1989), Are U.K. stock prices excessively volatile? Trading rules and variance bounds tests, *The Economic Journal.*

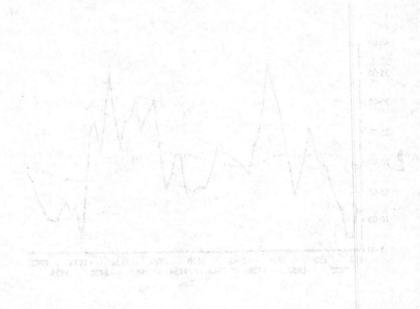

Chapter 5

Volatility of Prices and Volatility of Dividends *

The theoretical model which we present in this chapter is an attempt to develop a framework of analysis sufficiently general to study the volatility of stock prices when markets are efficient but with no a priori specification on the distribution of the relevant stochastic processes. To this aim, we shift the attention from dividends to earnings and we take as the exogenous source of uncertainty the innovation in the present discounted value of earnings. We use the following notation in the rest of this chapter: p_t and d_t are the price and dividend per share at time t, N_t is the number of shares outstanding at time t, X_t is total earnings and B_t is debt at time t. The (fixed) interest rate will be denoted by r and the discount factor by $\gamma = (1+r)^{-1}$. We will use the notation e_t to indicate the innovation in the present discounted value of earnings per share, i.e.

$$ N_{t-1} e_t = \left(E_t - E_{t-1} \right) \sum_{\tau=t}^{\infty} \frac{X_\tau}{(1+r)^{\tau-t}}. $$

As any innovation process, the stochastic process defining e_t satisfies

$$ E(e_t) = 0 \quad , \quad \forall t $$

and

$$ cov(e_t, e_s) = 0 \quad , \quad \forall t \neq s $$

We make the following assumption:

---

* Chapter based on a joint research with Margaret Bray (see Bray and Marseguerra, 1996).

ASSUMPTION 5.1

The stochastic process defining e_t is variance stationary, i.e.

$$Var(e_t) = \sigma_e^2 \quad , \quad \forall t$$

Notice that this assumption is perfectly compatible with earnings being a (nonstationary) random walk, as usually assumed in finance literature. [29]

The length of time for which innovations in earnings affect prices and dividends will be denoted by n; m will be the forecast horizon and T will be the sample length.

PROPOSITION 5.1

If the stochastic process of price per share, p_t, and dividend per share, d_t, is compatible, for all t, with the expected present value relation

$$p_t = E_t \left(\frac{p_{t+1} + d_{t+1}}{1 + r} \right) \tag{5.1}$$

with the sources and uses of funds identity

$$X_t + B_t + (N_t - N_{t-1})p_t = (1 + r)B_{t-1} + N_{t-1}d_t \tag{5.2}$$

---

[29] The random walk characterization of annual earnings has been supported by time-series analysis and forecasting studies such as those by Ball and Watts (1972) and Watts and Lefwich (1977). For a more recent analysis, see Ali and Zarowin (1992). If earnings are a random walk, i.e. in terms of deviation from mean,

$$X_t = X_{t-1} + \epsilon_t$$

then the definition of innovation in pdv of earnings implies

$$N_{t-1} e_t = (1 + r)\epsilon_t / r$$

and with the transversality conditions that, for all t,

$$\lim_{m \to \infty} E_t \left(\frac{N_{t+m}\, p_{t+m} + B_{t+m}}{(1+r)^{m-t}} \right) = 0 \tag{5.3}$$

and the limit exists

$$\lim_{m \to \infty} E_t \left(\sum_{\tau=t+1}^{m} \frac{X_\tau}{(1+r)^{\tau-t}} \right)$$

then

$$p_{t+1} + d_{t+1} = (1+r)p_t + e_{t+1} \tag{5.4}$$

where e_{t+1} is the innovation in the present value of earnings per share at $t+1$.

Proof: see Appendix

Proposition 5.1 allows us to gain several important insights on the behaviour of prices and dividends when the market is efficient by assumption. Before discussing the theoretical implications of the above Proposition, a brief review of some empirical findings on real prices and dividends is worthwhile.

Empirically aggregate real stock prices are fairly high correlated over time with aggregate real dividends. For example, for the annual (January) real $S\&P$'s composite stock price index and the corresponding annual real dividend series between 1926 and 1983 the simple correlation coefficient is 0.91. Of course, part of this correlation is due to a common trend between the two series, and yet the correlation of prices with time over the same sample is only 0.60. Thus, the price of the aggregate stock market is importantly linked to its dividends and much of the movement of the stock market can be traced to movements in dividends. However, although the correlation coefficient between prices and dividends is fairly high, the real prices is substantially more volatile than the real dividend. If price is regressed on dividend with a constant term in 1926-1983 sample period, the coefficient of dividends is 38.0 and the constant term is -0.28.

It has sometimes been argued that this extreme volatility of stock prices relative to dividends is clear evidence of overreaction of prices to dividends, and to explain this as well as other market's anomalies, like the perverse behaviour of the price/earnings ratio, several fads or changing fashion theories have been put forward (see, e.g., Shiller, 1989). Proposition 1 can be used to shed new light on this issue. Taking variances in eq.(5.4) and assuming variance stationarity for prices and dividends, we obtain

$$\sigma_p^2 + 2\rho_{pd}\,\sigma_p\,\sigma_d + \sigma_d^2 = (1+r)^2\sigma_p^2 + \sigma_e^2 \qquad (5.5)$$

where ρ_{pd} is the correlation coefficient between prices and dividends. Eq.(5.5) is an hyperbola in the (σ_d, σ_p)-plan and fig. 3, page 73, shows this curve for different values of $\rho \in [0,1]$ [30]. These plots show clearly how uncertainty in earnings goes into volatility of prices and dividends in a market efficient by assumption. To further investigate the consequences of Proposition 1, we will examine the two polar cases $\rho = 1$ and $\rho = -1$, i.e. when prices and dividends are perfectly correlated. Fig. 4, page 73, shows the two lines of the hyperbolas corresponding to a correlation coefficient of 1 (lower curve) and -1 (upper curve), both obviously restricted to the positive quadrant. [31] When prices and dividends are perfectly correlated, we have (in terms of deviation from mean)

$$p_{t+1} = \mu d_{t+1} \qquad (5.6)$$

with positive (negative) correlation for positive (negative) values of μ. From (5.4) and (5.6) we obtain, for $\mu \neq 0$,

$$p_{t+1} = \mu\Big(\frac{1+r}{1+\mu}\Big)p_t + \Big(\frac{\mu}{1+\mu}\Big)e_{t+1} \qquad (5.7)$$

---

[30] Eq.(5.5) is also an hyperbola in the (σ_p^2, σ_d^2)-space for most of the values of r and ρ but unfortunately not for all such values. To avoid unnecessary complications, we skip a detailed analysis of the conic in eq.(5.5) in the otherwise more appealing space of variances. The conclusion in text are not affected by this choice of space.

[31] If $\sigma_e^2 = 0$, then the hyperbola in eq.(5.5) splits up into two lines through origin.

and

$$d_{t+1} = \mu\left(\frac{1+r}{1+\mu}\right) d_t + \left(\frac{1}{1+\mu}\right) e_{t+1} \qquad (5.8)$$

while, for $\mu = 0$, prices are constant and dividends reduces to a zero mean white noise. If prices and dividends are to be stationary we require

$$-1 < \mu\left(\frac{1+r}{1+\mu}\right) < 1$$

i.e.

$$-\left(\frac{1}{2+r}\right) < \mu < \frac{1}{r} \qquad (5.9)$$

Variances are given, for $\mu \neq 0$, by

$$Var(p_t) = \sigma_p^2 = \frac{\sigma_e^2}{(1 + \frac{1}{\mu})^2 - (1+r)^2} \qquad (5.10)$$

and

$$Var(d_t) = \sigma_d^2 = \frac{\sigma_e^2}{\mu^2[(1 + \frac{1}{\mu})^2 - (1+r)^2]} \qquad (5.11)$$

while, for $\mu = 0$, $Var(d_t) = \sigma_e^2$ and $Var(p_t) = 0$. From eq (5.10) is immediately evident that σ_p^2 is decreasing when μ lies in the interval $(-\frac{1}{2+r}, 0)$ and is increasing when μ is in the interval $(0, \frac{1}{r})$. Also, for $\mu = 0$, $\sigma_p^2 = 0$. Similarly, from eq.(5.11) we have that σ_d^2 has a minimum for $\mu = \mu^* = \frac{1}{r^2 + 2r}$ and is decreasing for $\mu \in (-\frac{1}{2+r}, \mu^*)$ and is increasing for $\mu \in (\mu^*, \frac{1}{r})$. For $\mu = 0$, $\sigma_d^2 = \sigma_e^2$.

We can summarize the above analysis with the aid of fig. 4 which, as explained, shows the two hyperbolas for $\rho = 1$ and $\rho = -1$. On the upper curve, prices and dividends are perfectly correlated ($\mu < 0$) and as μ tends to $-\frac{1}{2+r}$, the corresponding point A in the (σ_p, σ_d)-space goes infinitely far from the origin along the curve. $\mu = 0$ corresponds to point B. As far as economics is concerned, the piece of the curve below point B is most interesting. When moving from B to C, there is a trade-off between standard deviations of prices and dividends: when selecting

μ in $(0, \mu^*)$, managers are effectively trading off variance in dividends with variance in prices. A smooth dividend policy, with small response of dividends to news (accomplished by choosing μ close to μ^*) is associated to high variance of prices. If instead μ is greater than μ^*, then no such trade-off is now possible and points in the (σ_p, σ_d)-space corresponding to such values of μ attain high variance of both prices and dividends. Overall, for $\mu > 0$, σ_p is unambiguously increasing, while σ_d is at first decreasing (for $\mu \in (0, \mu^*)$) and then increasing (for $\mu \in (\mu^*, \frac{1}{r})$). The last result can be better explained if we compare eq.(5.7) and eq.(5.8): for any value of μ, a fraction $\frac{\mu}{1+\mu}$ of the shock in earnings goes into prices and a fraction $\frac{1}{1+\mu}$ goes into dividends. When μ is positive but only slightly, most of the shock in earnings goes into dividends: between B and C the dominant effect is the reduction in $\frac{1}{1+\mu}e_{t+1}$ and so σ_d decreases. On the other hand, when μ is close to $\frac{1}{r}$, the response of dividends to earnings is small and most of the shock goes into prices: between C and D the dominant effect is the increase in $\mu\frac{1+r}{1+\mu}d_t$ and so σ_d increases (small but persistent shock in dividends). Finally, note that the two extreme cases of μ very close to $-\frac{1}{2+r}$ or to $\frac{1}{r}$ correspond both to a (quasi) random walk in prices and dividends: extremely smooth dividend policy with high variance of both prices and dividends, very small response of dividends to news but big reaction of prices to news.

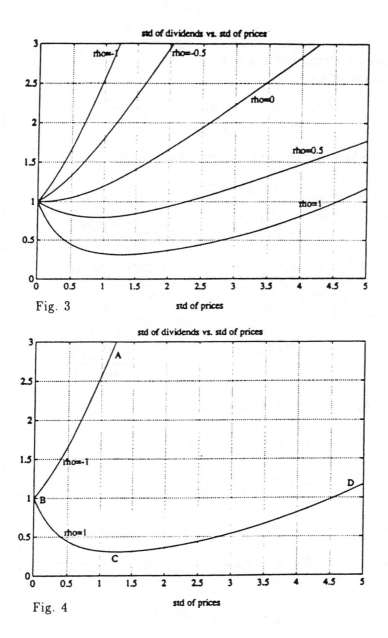

Fig. 3

Fig. 4

Appendix

Proof of Proposition 5.1

Equation (5.1) implies that

$$(1+r)N_\tau\, p_\tau = E_\tau\left[N_{\tau+1}p_{\tau+1} - (N_{\tau+1} - N_\tau)p_{\tau+1} + \right.$$
$$\left. + N_\tau\, d_{\tau+1}\right] \qquad (A5.1)$$

so from the law of iterated expectations, $\forall \tau \geq t$,

$$E_t(N_\tau\, p_\tau) = E_t\left[\frac{N_{\tau+1}p_{\tau+1}}{1+r}\right] +$$
$$+ E_t\left[\frac{N_\tau\, d_{\tau+1} - (N_{\tau+1} - N_\tau)p_{\tau+1}}{1+r}\right] \qquad (A5.2)$$

dividing by $(1+r)^{\tau-t}$ and summing implies that

$$\sum_{\tau=t}^{m} \frac{E_t(N_\tau\, p_\tau)}{(1+r)^{\tau-t}} = E_t\left[\sum_{\tau=t+1}^{m+1} \frac{N_\tau\, p_\tau}{(1+r)^{\tau-t}}\right] +$$
$$+ E_t\left[\sum_{\tau=t+1}^{m+1} \frac{N_{\tau-1}d_\tau - (N_\tau - N_{\tau-1})p_\tau}{(1+r)^{\tau-t}}\right] \qquad (A5.3)$$

so, as $E_t(N_t p_t) = N_t p_t$, we obtain

$$N_t p_t = E_t\left[\frac{N_{m+1}p_{m+1}}{(1+r)^{m+1-t}}\right] +$$
$$+ E_t\left[\sum_{\tau=t+1}^{m+1} \frac{N_{\tau-1}d_\tau - (N_\tau - N_{\tau-1})p_\tau}{(1+r)^{\tau-t}}\right] \qquad (A5.4)$$

Now, eq.(A5.4), replacing t by $t+1$, implies that

$$N_t(p_{t+1} + d_{t+1}) = N_{t+1}p_{t+1} + N_t d_{t+1} - (N_{t+1} - N_t)p_{t+1}$$

i.e.

$$N_t(p_{t+1} + d_{t+1}) = E_{t+1}\left[\frac{N_{m+1}p_{m+1}}{(1+r)^{m-t}}\right] +$$
$$+ E_{t+1}\left[\sum_{\tau=t+1}^{m+1} \frac{N_{\tau-1}d_\tau - (N_\tau - N_{\tau-1})p_\tau}{(1+r)^{\tau-t-1}}\right] \qquad (A5.5)$$

so that, from (A5.4) and (A5.5), we have

$$N_t[(1+r)p_t - p_{t+1} - d_{t+1}] = (E_t - E_{t+1})\left[\frac{N_{m+1}p_{m+1}}{(1+r)^{m-t}} + \right.$$

$$\left. + \sum_{\tau=t+1}^{m+1} \frac{N_{\tau-1}d_\tau - (N_\tau - N_{\tau-1})p_\tau}{(1+r)^{\tau-t-1}}\right]$$

$$(A5.6)$$

But from the sources and uses of funds we have

$$\sum_{\tau=t+1}^{m+1} \frac{N_{\tau-1}d_\tau - (N_\tau - N_{\tau-1})p_\tau}{(1+r)^{\tau-t-1}} = \sum_{\tau=t+1}^{m+1} \frac{X_\tau + B_\tau - (1+r)B_{\tau-1}}{(1+r)^{\tau-t-1}}$$

i.e.

$$\sum_{\tau=t+1}^{m+1} \frac{N_{\tau-1}d_\tau - (N_\tau - N_{\tau-1})p_\tau}{(1+r)^{\tau-t-1}} = \sum_{\tau=t+1}^{m+1} \frac{X_\tau}{(1+r)^{\tau-t-1}} +$$

$$+ \frac{B_{m+1}}{(1+r)^{m-t}} - (1+r)B_t \qquad (A5.7)$$

Thus, from (A5.6) and (A5.7), as $E_t B_t = E_{t+1} B_t$, we have

$$N_t[(1+r)p_t - p_{t+1} - d_{t+1}] = (E_t - E_{t+1})\left[\sum_{\tau=t+1}^{m+1} \frac{X_\tau}{(1+r)^{\tau-t-1}} + \right.$$

$$\left. + \frac{B_{m+1}}{(1+r)^{m-t}} - (1+r)B_t + \frac{N_{m+1}p_{m+1}}{(1+r)^{m-t}}\right]$$

i.e.

$$N_t[(1+r)p_t - p_{t+1} - d_{t+1}] = (E_t - E_{t+1})\left[\sum_{\tau=t+1}^{m+1} \frac{X_\tau}{(1+r)^{\tau-t-1}} + \right.$$

$$\left. + \frac{B_{m+1} + N_{m+1}p_{m+1}}{(1+r)^{m-t}}\right]$$

and, finally,

$$N_t[(1+r)p_t - p_{t+1} - d_{t+1}] = (E_t - E_{t+1})\left[\sum_{\tau=t+1}^{\infty} \frac{X_\tau}{(1+r)^{\tau-t-1}}\right]$$

$$= -N_t e_{t+1} \qquad (A5.8)$$

where the last equality is obtained taking limit for $m \to +\infty$ and using the transversality condition. Eq.(A5.8) proves the result.

Chapter 6

A General Framework for the Variance Bounds Inequality [*]

6.1 Expected Sample Variance of Prices

Suppose now that agents have sufficient information to fore-cast dividends perfectly up to period m (and so assume $m \geq t$, $\forall t = 1, \ldots, T$) and let us define p^*_{mt} in the following way:

$$p^*_{mt} = \sum_{\tau=t+1}^{m} \frac{d_\tau}{(1+r)^{\tau-t}} + \frac{p_m}{(1+r)^{m-t}} \qquad (6.1)$$

Notice that Shiller's ex post perfect foresight price is a limiting case (for $m = \infty$) of (6.1). Also, the approximation usually used of the ex post rational price to implement operational tests of the variance bounds inequality, is obtained by setting in (6.1) $m = T$. As a straightforward consequence of Proposition 5.1, we have the following corollary:

COROLLARY 6.1

Let p^*_{mt} be defined by eq.(6.1). Then

$$p^*_{mt} = p_t + \sum_{\tau=t+1}^{m} \frac{e_\tau}{(1+r)^{\tau-t}}$$

---

[*] Chapter based on a joint research with Margaret Bray (see Bray and Marseguerra, 1996).

Proof: From (5.4) we have

$$\sum_{\tau=t+1}^{m} \frac{p_\tau}{(1+r)^{\tau-t}} + \sum_{\tau=t+1}^{m} \frac{d_\tau}{(1+r)^{\tau-t}} = \sum_{\tau=t}^{m-1} \frac{p_\tau}{(1+r)^{\tau-t}} +$$
$$+ \sum_{\tau=t+1}^{m} \frac{e_\tau}{(1+r)^{\tau-t}}$$

i.e.

$$\frac{p_m}{(1+r)^{m-t}} + \sum_{\tau=t+1}^{m} \frac{d_\tau}{(1+r)^{\tau-t}} = p_t + \sum_{\tau=t+1}^{m} \frac{e_\tau}{(1+r)^{\tau-t}}$$

which proves the result.

In order to derive a general formula for the expected sample variance of p_t and p_{mt}^*, we need the following Proposition:

PROPOSITION 6.1

Suppose $N = N_t = N_{t+1} = \ldots$ (i.e. there is no issue of shares at or after date t). Then, for any $(n+1)$-vector of real numbers $a = (a_0, a_1, \ldots, a_n)'$, any price per share at date t, p_t, and any level of debt at date t, B_t, there is a dividend per share policy given by

$$d_\tau = rc + (1+r)y_{\tau-1} - y_\tau + e_\tau \qquad , \qquad \forall \tau > t \qquad (6.2)$$

where

$$y_\tau = \sum_{i=0}^{n} a_i e_{\tau-i} \qquad (6.3)$$

and

$$c = \frac{1}{N}\left[E_t\left(\sum_{i=t+1}^{\infty} \frac{X_i}{(1+r)^{i-t}} \right) - B_t \right] - y_t \qquad (6.4)$$

which results in a price process

$$p_\tau = c + \sum_{i=0}^{n} a_i e_{\tau-i} = c + y_\tau \qquad (6.5)$$

which satisfies both the expected present value requirement

$$E_{\tau-1}[p_\tau + d_\tau] = (1+r)p_{\tau-1} \quad , \quad \forall \tau > t \quad (6.6)$$

and the Modigliani-Miller theorem that

$$B_\tau + Np_\tau = E_\tau\Big[\sum_{i=\tau+1}^{\infty} \frac{X_i}{(1+r)^{i-\tau}} \Big] \quad , \quad \forall \tau \geq t \quad (6.7)$$

Proof: see Appendix

We generalize the last Proposition slightly by adding a random walk term to dividends in eq. (6.2), i.e. let now

$$d_\tau = rc + (1+r)y_{\tau-1} - y_\tau + e_\tau + r\beta\Big(\sum_{i=1}^{\tau-1} e_{i-n}\Big).$$

where β is a (real) random walk parameter. This puts a random walk component in prices, i.e. prices become

$$\hat{p}_\tau = c + y_\tau + \beta\Big(\sum_{i=1}^{\tau-1} e_{i-n}\Big)$$

The expected present value requirement is still satisfied and whether or not this random walk term in dividends is possible without debt getting unbounded depends on the expected present value of earnings, i.e.

$$E_t\Big[\sum_{\tau=t+1}^{\infty} \frac{X_\tau}{(1+r)^\tau} \Big] \quad ;$$

if this includes a random walk term, then a random walk term in prices and dividends is possible without debt becoming unbounded. In what follows, we will allow both for stationary and non stationary prices in accordance with , respectively, $\beta = 0$ and $\beta \neq 0$.

From Proposition 2 we know that it is possible to set a dividend policy which results in a price process

$$p_t = c + \sum_{i=0}^{n} a_i e_{t-i} + \beta \left(\sum_{i=1}^{t-1} e_{i-n} \right) \tag{6.8}$$

and from Corollary 1 we also know that p^*_{mt} as defined in equation (6.1) satisfies

$$p^*_{mt} = p_t + \sum_{\tau=t+1}^{m} \frac{e_\tau}{(1+r)^{\tau-t}} \tag{6.9}$$

Defining now the new vector α by

$$\alpha = \begin{pmatrix} a \\ \beta \end{pmatrix} \quad,$$

for $t = 1, 2, \ldots, T$ let

$$q_{mnt}(\gamma, \alpha) = \sum_{\tau=t+1}^{m} e_\tau \gamma^{\tau-t} + \sum_{i=0}^{n} a_i e_{t-i} + \beta \left(\sum_{i=1}^{t-1} e_{i-n} \right) \tag{6.10}$$

Comparing (6.8), (6.9) and (6.10) it follows that

$$p_t = c + q_{mnt}(0, \alpha)$$

and

$$p^*_{mt} = c + q_{mnt}(\gamma, \alpha)$$

and in matrix form

$$q_{mn}(\gamma, \alpha) = Be \tag{6.11}$$

where

$$q_{mn}(\gamma, \alpha) = \begin{pmatrix} q_{mn1}(\gamma, \alpha) \\ \vdots \\ q_{mnT}(\gamma, \alpha) \end{pmatrix} \quad, \qquad e = \begin{pmatrix} e_m \\ e_{m-1} \\ \vdots \\ e_0 \\ e_{-1} \\ \vdots \\ e_{-n+1} \end{pmatrix}$$

and B is the $T \times (m+n)$ matrix

$$B =$$

$$
\begin{pmatrix}
\gamma^{m-1} & \cdots & \gamma^{T-1} & \cdots & \gamma^{T-n-2} & \cdots & a_0 & \cdots & a_n \\
\vdots & \ddots & \vdots & \ddots & \vdots & \ddots & \vdots & \ddots & \vdots \\
\gamma^{m-T+1} & \cdots & \gamma & \cdots & a_n & \cdots & \beta & \cdots & \beta \\
\gamma^{m-T} & \cdots & a_0 & \cdots & \beta & \cdots & \beta & \cdots & \beta
\end{pmatrix}
$$

i.e.

$$
b_{ij} = \begin{cases}
\gamma^{m+1-i-j}, & \text{if } i+j \le m \text{ ;} \\
a_{i+j-m-1}, & \text{if } m+i \le i+j \le m+n-1 \text{ ;} \\
\beta, & \text{if } i+j < m+n+1 \text{ .}
\end{cases}
$$

We are now ready to derive a general formula for the expected sample variance of both $\{p_t\}_{t=1}^{T}$ and $\{p_t^*\}_{t=1}^{T}$. From eq.(6.11) we write the expected sample variance of $q_{mnT}(\gamma, \alpha)$ as a constant times the sum of the sample variances of the columns of the matrix B. More precisely, as explained in the Appendix, we have the following expression for the expected sample variance of $q_{mn}(\gamma, \alpha)$:

$$
V_{mnt}(\gamma, \alpha) \stackrel{\text{def}}{=} E\left\{ \frac{1}{T}\sum_{t=1}^{T} [q_{mnt}(\gamma, \alpha)]^2 - \left[\frac{1}{T}\sum_{t=1}^{T} q_{mnt}(\gamma, \alpha)\right]^2 \right\}
$$

$$
= \sigma_e^2 \sum_{i=1}^{m+n} \left[\frac{(b_i' b_i)}{T} - \frac{(1' b_i)^2}{T^2} \right] \tag{6.12}
$$

Moreover, after some little algebra (see again Appendix for details), eq.(6.12) reduces to a quadratic form, i.e. [32]

$$
V_{mnT}(\gamma, a, \beta) = \sigma_e^2 [h(\gamma, m, T) + g'Hg - 2a'Kg + a'La \\
+ \phi\beta^2 - 2\beta(y'a + z'g)] \tag{6.13}
$$

where

$$
h(\gamma, m, T) = \frac{\gamma^2(1 - \gamma^{2(m-T)})}{1 - \gamma^2} \left[\frac{1}{T}\left(\frac{1 - \gamma^{2T}}{1 - \gamma^2}\right) - \frac{1}{T^2}\left(\frac{1 - \gamma^T}{1 - \gamma}\right)^2 \right] ,
$$

---

[32] To keep notation as simple as possible, we will assume throughout $T > n+2$. This assumption seems quite reasonable.

g is the $(T-1)$-vector given by

$$g' = (\gamma^{T-1} \quad \cdots \quad \gamma) \,,$$

H is a $(T-1) \times (T-1)$-matrix such that

$$H_{ij} = \begin{cases} (\frac{1}{T} - \frac{1}{T^2})i, & \text{for } i = j \,; \\ -\frac{1}{T^2}min(i,j), & \text{for } i \neq j, \end{cases}$$

K is a $(n+1) \times (T-1)$-matrix such that

$$k_{ij} = \frac{1}{T^2}max(j - i + 1, 0) \,,$$

L is a $(n+1) \times (n+1)$-matrix such that

$$L_{ij} = \begin{cases} 1 - \frac{1}{T}, & \text{for } i = j \,; \\ -\frac{1}{T^2}[T - |i - j|], & \text{for } i \neq j. \end{cases}$$

the $(n+1)$-vector y is given by

$$y_j = \frac{1}{2T^2}(T - n - 2 + j)(T - n - 1 + j) \qquad , \qquad 1 \leq j \leq n + 1$$

the $(T-1)$-vector z is given by

$$z_j = \begin{cases} 0, & \text{for } j \leq n + 1 \,; \\ \frac{1}{2T^2}(j - n)(j - n - 1), & \text{for } j \geq n + 2. \end{cases}$$

and, finally,

$$\phi = \sum_{i=1}^{T-1} (\frac{i}{T} - \frac{i^2}{T^2}) = \frac{T^2 - 1}{6T}$$

As a final piece of notation, notice that equation (6.13) can be rewritten as

$$V_{mnT}(\gamma, \alpha) = \sigma_e^2 [h(\gamma, m, T) + g'Hg - 2\alpha'\hat{K}g + \alpha'\hat{L}\alpha] \qquad (6.13)'$$

where

$$\hat{K} = \begin{pmatrix} K \\ z' \end{pmatrix}$$

and

$$\hat{L} = \begin{pmatrix} L & -y \\ -y' & \phi \end{pmatrix}$$

6.2 Grossness of a Violation

The question we now want to answer is when we should expect to find "excess volatility" of prices. The analysis developed so far allows to derive a general formulation for the variance bound violations. With the notation introduced, we have an expected violation of the variance bound when, for $\theta \in (0, 1)$,

$$V_{mnT}(\gamma, \alpha) \leq \theta V_{mnT}(0, \alpha) \qquad (6.14)$$

As explained above, the LHS of (6.14) represents the expected sample variance of $\{p_t^*\}_{t=1}^T$, and the RHS is θ times the expected sample variance of $\{p_t\}_{t=1}^T$. There are two elements of interest in inequality (6.14) : the first is the parameter θ , which gives a measure of the violation and, second, the vector α of coefficients of $\{p_t^*\}_{t=1}^T$ and $\{p_t\}_{t=1}^T$ which satisfy the inequality. For each $\theta \in (0, 1)$ we can find a set of vectors $\alpha(\theta)$ such that (6.14) is satisfied. In particular, we are interested in determining the minimum $\theta \in (0, 1)$ for which the set of such $\alpha(\theta)$ is non-empty. The following proposition characterizes both such θ and $\alpha(\theta)$.

PROPOSITION 6.2

There exists a unique $\theta = \theta^* \in (0, 1)$, where

$$\theta^* = 1 - \frac{g'\hat{K}'\hat{L}^{-1}\hat{K}g}{h(\gamma, m, T) + g'Hg} \qquad , \qquad (6.15)$$

such that θ^* is the minimum value of $\theta \in (0, 1)$ for which exists some $\alpha(\theta)$ satisfying the inequality (6.14). Moreover, $\alpha(\theta^*)$ is unique and given by

$$\alpha(\theta^*) = \left[\frac{h(\gamma, m, T) + g'Hg}{g'\hat{K}'\hat{L}^{-1}\hat{K}g} \right] \hat{L}^{-1}\hat{K}g \qquad (6.16)$$

and for $\theta = \theta^*$ and $\alpha = \alpha(\theta^*)$ inequality (6.14) holds as an equality.

Proof : See Appendix

The above Proposition allows us to define the expected *grossness* of a violation as

$$g_{mnT} = \frac{1}{\theta^*} = \left[\frac{h(\gamma, m, T) + g'Hg - g'\hat{K}'\hat{L}^{-1}\hat{K}g}{h(\gamma, m, T) + g'Hg} \right]^{-1} \quad (6.17)$$

The following Proposition (whose formal proof is given, as usual, in the Appendix) summarize the main properties of the concept of grossness of a violation:

PROPOSITION 6.3

i) For a given sample length, T, and for a given forecast horizon, m, the grossness g_{mnT} of a violation, as defined in eq.(6.17), is increasing in n (see Fig. 5 and 7, page 88 and 89, respectively).

ii) for a given n (number of lags affecting the present) and a given m (forecast horizon), g_{mnT} is decreasing in T (see Fig 6 and 7, page 88 and 89, respectively).

iii) for a given n (number of lags affecting the present and a given T (sample length) g_{mnT} is decreasing in m (see Fig 8, page 89).

Proof: see Appendix

The intuition for the findings of the above Proposition lies in the discussion in §4.2 about the downward bias of estimates of sample variances based on sample means rather than population means. First, it is obvious that this effect is reduced by increasing T. However, changing m or n also results in a change of the correlation of both p_t and p_t^* and what the Proposition describes is the overall effect of this change.

In addition to the findings of the Proposition, results of numerical simulations suggest (see Fig 5, 6 and 8) that, as far as stationarity is concerned, violations are larger for prices with a random walk component ($\beta \neq 0$) than for stationary prices ($\beta = 0$). This is in accord with the well known result that finite sample bias is worsened by the presence of a unit root. Also (see Fig 5), the rate of increase of g_{mnT} with respect to n is much larger for stationary prices and dividends than for the random walk component case. Figures 9 and 10, page 90, plot two two different realizations of prices and perfect foresight prices for the economy described in this Chapter (stationary case, i.e. $\beta = 0$, $T = m = 100$, $n = 90$, $r = 0.05$). [33] The relevant characteristics of these plots are very similar to those in Figures 1 and 2 corresponding to real data, for the U.S. and U.K. market respectively. From Figures 9 and 10 (and, similarly, from Fig. 11 and 12) the bound (4.7) would seem clearly violated and, consequently, the valuation model (4.4) untenable. However, as we know, these plots are based on (simulated) data that by construction are generated by the rational valuation model (4.4). The rational model developed in this Chapter is therefore able to reproduce quite well (both for stationary and nonstationary prices and dividends) plots very similar to those used by Shiller to claim the failure of the efficient market hypothesis. There is a difference, however. In Figures 13 and 14, page 92, we plot the grossness of the violation for 300 realizations of the economy (same parameters' values as before): the grossness of the violation is clearly smaller than that originally obtained by Shiller. This leaves the problem of the determination of prices in real world a puzzle and somehow strengthens the original conclusions of Shiller. [34]

---

[33] The same argument applies to Figures 11 and 12, page 91, which are obtained for the same set of values of the parameters but for the nonstationary case.

[34] It would have been interesting to obtain some idea about the possible shape of the distribution of the grossness. Unfortunately this is not easily obtained (even if we restrict ourselves to numerical results) because it would require extremely long (i.e. time consuming) computations. Indeed, because of the well known fact that the expected

6.3 Conclusion

For over than thirteen years since Shiller (1981) and LeRoy and Porter (1981), economists have tried to understand the original finding of excess volatility of stock prices. After assuming a given stochastic process for dividends, they have tried to derive implications for rationally set prices and then tested these implications for real data. The general impression from these tests is that, although the original results were subject to problems of small sample bias and nonstationarity that may have affected the magnitude of the findings of excessive volatility, when these difficulties are tackled excess volatility is still found, even if of an order of magnitude smaller than first obtained.

In this Part of the book we attempted to answer a different question, i.e. what is the response of dividend policy to shocks in the present discounted value of earnings. We shifted the attention from dividends to earnings as an exogenous source of uncertainty and showed how there is a fundamental trade-off between volatility of prices and volatility of dividends. Dividend smoothing policies basically exploit this trade-off.

We also derived a new framework to explore the relationship between dividend and prices and to analyze excess volatility of prices. This is done with the model developed in this Chapter. We fully characterized conditions leading to "excess" volatility and showed that a rational market is perfectly compatible with most of the Shiller's findings. Our framework is sufficiently general to allow for both stationary and nonstationary prices and dividends. This is particularly important, because most of the debate which followed the Shiller and LeRoy and Porter papers has focused on the issue of nonstationarity of the relevant stochastic processes. As pointed out by Merton (1987b) (see also §4.2 above), variance bound tests can help in clarifying the issue of market rationality only if the level of rationally determined real and detrended stock

---

value of a ratio is not the same as the ratio of the expected values, we should repeat several times the, say, 300, realizations of the economy and we will then obtain just one single number from each sequence of simulations.

prices can be described by a stationary process. Unfortunately, up to now the empirical evidence on the temporal stability of dividends and stock prices is far from conclusive. and more theoretical work on the impact of earnings changes on dividend policy and prices seems therefore appropriate. The work here presented is a first step in this direction.

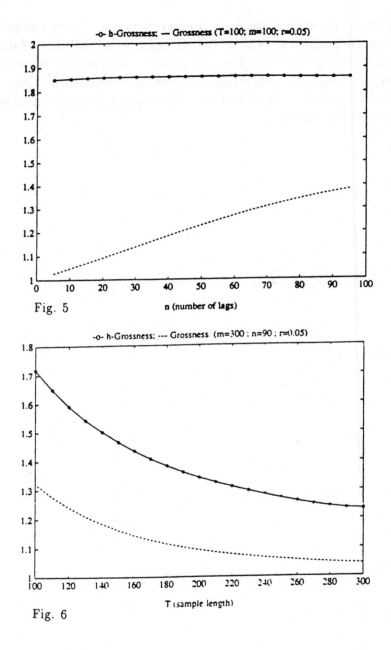

Fig. 5

Fig. 6

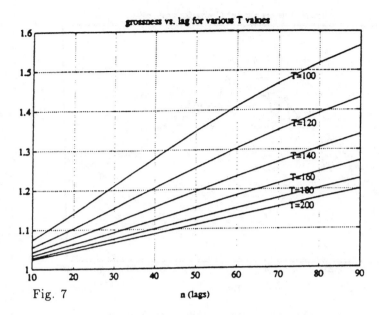

Fig. 7

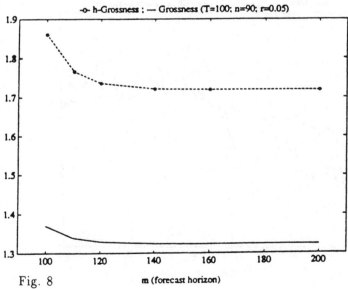

Fig. 8

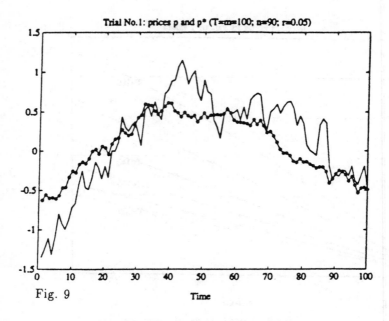

Fig. 9

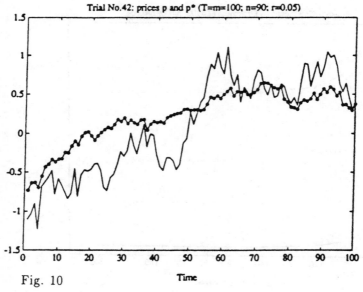

Fig. 10

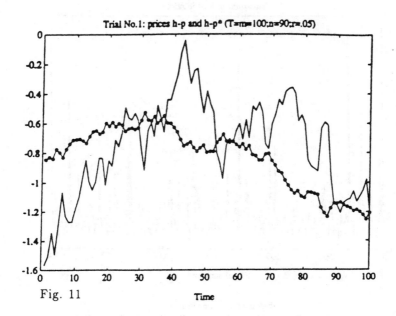

Fig. 11

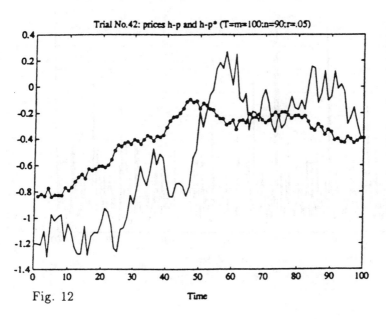

Fig. 12

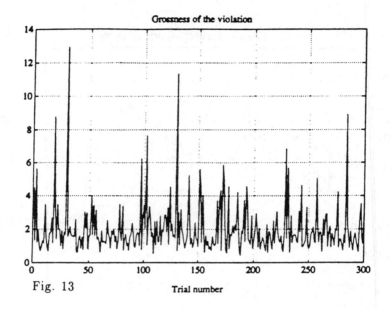

Fig. 13

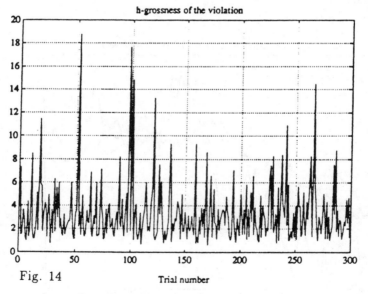

Fig. 14

Appendix

Proof of Proposition 6.1

From eqs (4.2) and (4.5) we have, $\forall \tau > t$,

$$p_\tau + d_\tau = (1+r)(c + y_{\tau-1}) + e_\tau$$

i.e.

$$p_\tau + d_\tau = (1+r)p_{\tau-1} + e_\tau$$

so, as e_τ is an innovation,

$$E_{\tau-1}[p_\tau + d_\tau] = (1+r)p_{\tau-1}$$

which establishes (4.6). Now, for $\tau = t$ (4.7) follows immediately from (4.4) and (4.5). For $\tau > t$, from (4.2) and (4.5) we have

$$\sum_{i=t+1}^{\tau} \frac{d_i}{(1+r)^{i-t}} = c\left[1 - \left(\frac{1}{1+r}\right)^{\tau-t}\right] + y_t - \frac{y_\tau}{(1+r)^{\tau-t}} +$$

$$+ \sum_{i=t+1}^{\tau} \frac{e_i}{(1+r)^{i-t}}$$

i.e.

$$\sum_{i=t+1}^{\tau} \frac{d_i}{(1+r)^{i-t}} = p_t - \frac{1}{(1+r)^{\tau-t}}p_\tau + \sum_{i=t+1}^{\tau} \frac{e_i}{(1+r)^{i-t}} \qquad (A6.1)$$

But from the sources and uses of funds identity we have, for $\forall \tau > t$,

$$\sum_{i=t+1}^{\tau} \frac{d_i}{(1+r)^{i-t}} = \frac{1}{N}\left[\sum_{i=t+1}^{\tau} \frac{X_i}{(1+r)^{i-t}} + \frac{B_\tau}{(1+r)^{\tau-t}} - B_t\right] \qquad (A6.2)$$

so from (A6.1) and (A6.2) we get

$$\frac{1}{N}\frac{B_\tau}{(1+r)^{\tau-t}} = p_t + \frac{B_t}{N} - \frac{1}{(1+r)^{\tau-t}}p_\tau +$$

$$+ \sum_{i=t+1}^{\tau} \frac{(e_i - X_i/N)}{(1+r)^{i-t}} \qquad (A6.3)$$

Now, from the definition of e_i, we have

$$\frac{e_i}{(1+r)^{i-t}} = \frac{1}{N}(E_i - E_{i-1})\Big(\sum_{j=i}^{\infty} \frac{X_j}{(1+r)^{j-t}}\Big)$$

and since $i \geq t+1$ and $(E_i - E_{i-1})X_j = 0 \; \forall j \leq i-1$, we can write

$$\frac{e_i}{(1+r)^{i-t}} = \frac{1}{N}(E_i - E_{i-1})\Big(\sum_{j=t+1}^{\infty} \frac{X_j}{(1+r)^{j-t}}\Big)$$

and therefore

$$\sum_{i=t+1}^{\tau} \frac{(e_i - X_i/N)}{(1+r)^{i-t}} = \frac{1}{N}\Big[E_\tau\Big(\sum_{j=t+1}^{\infty} \frac{X_j}{(1+r)^{j-t}}\Big) + $$
$$- E_t\Big(\sum_{j=t+1}^{\infty} \frac{X_j}{(1+r)^{j-t}}\Big) - \sum_{i=t+1}^{\tau} \frac{X_i}{(1+r)^{i-t}}\Big]$$

i.e

$$\sum_{i=t+1}^{\tau} \frac{(e_i - X_i/N)}{(1+r)^{i-t}} = \frac{1}{N}\Big[\frac{1}{(1+r)^{\tau-t}}E_\tau\Big(\sum_{i=\tau+1}^{\infty} \frac{X_i}{(1+r)^{i-\tau}}\Big) + $$
$$- E_t\Big(\sum_{j=t+1}^{\infty} \frac{X_j}{(1+r)^{j-t}}\Big)\Big]$$

$$(A6.4)$$

where to derive the last equality we used that

$$\sum_{i=t+1}^{\tau} \frac{X_i}{(1+r)^{i-t}}$$

is τ-measurable. From (A6.3) and (A6.4) and using (4.7) for $t = \tau$, we establish (4.7) for $\tau > t$.

Proof of Proposition 6.2

Let

$$V_{mnT\theta}(\gamma, \alpha) = V_{mnT}(\gamma, \alpha) - \theta V_{mnT}(0, \alpha) \qquad (A6.5)$$

We have to solve the following constrained optimization problem:

$$\min_{\theta \in (0,1)} \theta \qquad (A6.6)$$

s.t.

$$\min_{\alpha} V_{mnT\theta}(\gamma, \alpha) \leq 0$$

From elementary algebra we have, for each $\theta \in (0,1)$,

$$\min_{\alpha} V_{mnT\theta}(\gamma, \alpha) = h(\gamma, m, T) + g'Hg - \frac{1}{1-\theta} g'\hat{K}'\hat{L}^{-1}\hat{K}g \qquad (A6.7)$$

and

$$\alpha^*(\theta) = argmin\ V_{mnT\theta}(\gamma, \alpha) = \frac{1}{1-\theta}\hat{L}^{-1}\hat{K}g \qquad (A6.8)$$

Now, let

$$w_0 = h(\gamma, m, T) + g'Hg,$$
$$z_0 = g'\hat{K}'\hat{L}^{-1}\hat{K}g$$

and notice that

$$w_0 = V_{mnT}(\gamma, 0) > 0\ , \qquad (A6.9)$$

and since L is positive definite we also have

$$z_0 \geq 0 \qquad (A6.10)$$

Furthermore, since

$$w_0 - z_0 = \min_{\alpha} V_{mnT}(\gamma, \alpha)$$

it follows that (for $r > 0$)

$$w_0 - z_0 > 0 \qquad (A6.11)$$

The result now follows immediately from the study of the real function $f(\theta) = w_0 - z_0 \frac{1}{1-\theta}$ when conditions (A6.9), (A6.10) and (A6.11) are simultaneously satisfied.

Proof of Proposition 6.3

First of all, notice that decreasing n in the constrained minimization problem in Proposition 6.2 is equivalent to add new constraints (and precisely, if we move from n_2 to $n_1 < n_2$, then we add the constraints $a_{n_1+1} = a_{n_1+2} = \cdots = a_{n_2} = 0$) and so the corresponding new minimum value is greater than or equal to the previous one. Therefore, θ^* is decreasing with n and so g_{mnT} is increasing with n, and i) is proved.

Secondly, as far as ii) and iii) is concerned, notice that from (5.1) we have that

$$g_{mnT} = \max_{\alpha} \left[\frac{V_{mnT}(0, \alpha)}{V_{mnT}(\gamma, \alpha)} \right] \qquad (A6.12)$$

Now, increasing m (T) is equivalent to add a column (a row) in the matrix B in eq (4.11) and therefore the denominator in (A6.12) increases while the numerator stays the same. So g_{mnT} decreases and ii) and iii) are also proved.

Formal derivation of the expected sample variance formula

To derive formally the expected sample variance of $q_{mnT}(\gamma, \alpha)$, i.e. eqs. (6.13) and (6.13)', notice that from eq.(6.11) we have

$$\frac{1}{T} \sum_{t=1}^{T} [q_{mnt}(\gamma, \alpha)]^2 = \frac{1}{T} [q_{mn}(\gamma, \alpha)]' q_{mn}(\gamma, \alpha)$$

$$= \frac{1}{T} e' B' B e$$

$$= \frac{1}{T} tr(e' B' B e)$$

$$= \frac{1}{T} tr(B' B e e')$$

and using the properties of the stochastic process defining e_t we have

$$E\left\{\frac{1}{T}\sum_{t=1}^{T}[q_{mnt}(\gamma,\alpha)]^2\right\} = \frac{1}{T}tr[B'BE(ee')]$$

$$= \frac{\sigma_e^2}{T}tr(B'B)$$

$$= \frac{\sigma_e^2}{T}\sum_{i=1}^{m+n}(b_i'b_i) \qquad (A6.13)$$

where b_i is the i-th column of B. Similarly we have

$$\left[\frac{1}{T}\sum_{t=1}^{T}q_{mnt}(\gamma,\alpha)\right]^2 = \frac{1}{T^2}(1'q_{mn})^2$$

$$= \frac{1}{T^2}(1'Be)^2$$

and therefore

$$E\left[\frac{1}{T}\sum_{t=1}^{T}q_{mnt}(\gamma,\alpha)\right]^2 = \frac{1}{T^2}E(1'Bee'B'1)$$

$$= \frac{\sigma_e^2}{T^2}(1'BB'1)$$

$$= \frac{\sigma_e^2}{T^2}\sum_{i=1}^{m+n}(1'b_i)^2 \qquad (A6.14)$$

Putting together equations (A6.13) and (A6.14), we have the following expression for the expected sample variance of $q_{mn}(\gamma,\alpha)$:

$$V_{mnt}(\gamma,\alpha) \overset{\text{def}}{=} E\left\{\frac{1}{T}\sum_{t=1}^{T}[q_{mnt}(\gamma,\alpha)]^2 - \left[\frac{1}{T}\sum_{t=1}^{T}q_{mnt}(\gamma,\alpha)\right]^2\right\}$$

$$= \sigma_e^2 \sum_{i=1}^{m+n}\left[\frac{(b_i'b_i)}{T} - \frac{(1'b_i)^2}{T^2}\right] \qquad (A6.15)$$

In order to obtain an expression for $V_{mnt}(\gamma, \alpha)$, we will examine separately the first $m - T$ columns of B and then the remaining $n + T$ columns. For $i \leq m - T$, the i-th column of B is

$$
\begin{pmatrix} \gamma^{m-i} \\ \gamma^{m-i-1} \\ \vdots \\ \gamma^{m-i-T+1} \end{pmatrix} = \gamma^{m-i-T+1} \begin{pmatrix} \gamma^{T-1} \\ \gamma^{T-2} \\ \vdots \\ \gamma \\ 1 \end{pmatrix}
$$

in which case

$$
\frac{(b_i' b_i)}{T} - \frac{(1' b_i)^2}{T^2} = \gamma^{2(m-i-T+1)} \left[\frac{1}{T} \left(\frac{1 - \gamma^{2T}}{1 - \gamma^2} \right) - \frac{1}{T^2} \left(\frac{1 - \gamma^T}{1 - \gamma} \right)^2 \right]
$$

so that

$$
\sum_{i=1}^{m-T} \left[\frac{(b_i' b_i)}{T} - \frac{(1' b_i)^2}{T^2} \right] = \frac{\gamma^2 (1 - \gamma^{2(m-T)})}{1 - \gamma^2} \left[\frac{1}{T} \left(\frac{1 - \gamma^{2T}}{1 - \gamma^2} \right) + \right.
$$

$$
\left. - \frac{1}{T^2} \left(\frac{1 - \gamma^T}{1 - \gamma} \right)^2 \right]
$$

$$(A6.16)$$

where the RHS of equation (A6.16) has been defined in Section 6.1 as $h(\gamma, m, T)$. Let us now consider the remaining $n + T$ columns of the matrix B and, to simplify notation, let

$$
g' = (\gamma^{T-1} \quad \cdots \quad \gamma) \ , \quad b' = \overbrace{(\beta, \cdots, \beta)}^{T-1 \text{ times}}
$$

For each of these columns we have ($i = 1, 2, \ldots, n + T$)

$$
b_i = [O_{T,i-1}, I_T, O_{T,n+T-i}] \begin{pmatrix} g \\ a \\ b \end{pmatrix}
$$

so that

$$
b_i' b_i = (g', a', b') P \begin{pmatrix} g \\ a \\ b \end{pmatrix}
$$

where

$$P = \begin{pmatrix} O_{i-1} & O_{i-1,T} & O_{i-1,n+T-i} \\ O_{T,i-1} & I_T & O_{T,n+T-i} \\ O_{n+T-i,i-1} & O_{n+T-i,T} & O_{n+T-i} \end{pmatrix}$$

Therefore

$$\frac{1}{T} \sum_{i=1}^{n+T} b'_i b_i = \frac{1}{T} g' R g + a'a + \frac{\beta^2}{T} \left(\sum_{i=1}^{T-1} i \right) \qquad (A6.17)$$

where the elements of the $(T-1, T-1)$-matrix R are defined by

$$r_{ij} = \begin{cases} i, & \text{for } i = j \ ; \\ 0, & \text{for } i \neq j. \end{cases}$$

Similarly, we have

$$\frac{1}{T^2} \sum_{i=1}^{n+T} (1'b_i)^2 = \frac{1}{T^2} (g', a', b') S \begin{pmatrix} g \\ a \\ b \end{pmatrix} \qquad (A6.18)$$

where

$$S = \begin{pmatrix} S^{11}_{T-1} & S^{12}_{T-1,n+1} & S^{13}_{T-1} \\ S^{12'}_{T-1,n+1} & S^{22}_{n+1} & S^{23}_{n+1,T-1} \\ S^{13'}_{T-1} & S^{23'}_{n+1,T-1} & S^{33}_{T-1} \end{pmatrix}$$

and

$$S^{11}_{ij} = min(i,j)$$
$$S^{12}_{ij} = max(0, i+1-j)$$
$$S^{13}_{ij} = max[0, i-(j+n)]$$
$$S^{22}_{ij} = T - |i-j|$$
$$S^{23}_{ij} = max(0, T-n-1+i-j)$$
$$S^{33}_{ij} = T - max(i,j)$$

Eqs. (6.13) and (6.13)' now follow immediately from equations (A6.16), (A6.17) and (A6.18).

Part III

Ownership Structure and Investments

Chapter 7

Value, Ownership, and Equity Linkages

7.1 Introduction

In several industrialized countries, e.g. Japan, Italy and France, large quoted firms are connected through cross-shareholdings. Interlocking shareholding is not only a feature of corporate ownership, it is also an essential part of corporate governance in continental Europe and in Japan, and for this reason has attracted considerable interest in recent years. In many cases these ownership links are associated with the phenomenon of *business group*, i.e. a set of legally independent firms which are connected through shareholdings to achieve some form of coordination in running the business operations. There are essentially two types of business group (though the two forms of industrial organization sometimes overlap): The first *(the hierarchical group)* is common in continental Europe and is characterized by a pyramidal structure with a parent holding company on the top. Monitoring and decision-making are organized hierarchically and the firms of the group act as a single firm under the control of one main investor. The second *(the associative group)*, particularly popular in Japan with the name of *keiretsu* [35], consists of a number of firms based in different industries connected through equity linkages. Coordination of activities is obtained through more or less informal mechanisms, information exchanges and tacit rules of conduct. Why the system of corporate ownership and governance in the above mentioned countries takes on the form that it does is an intriguing issue. In fact, several different functions are performed by

---

[35] The term *keiretsu* is derived from the words *kei* meaning "faction or group" and *retsu* meaning "arranged in order" (see A. Viner, 1988, pg.2).

this form of financial organization for economic activities. First, in accordance with the transaction costs approach, it can be thought of as an intermediate form between market and hierarchy, being able to capture both some of the advantages deriving from market internalization (the transactions between group's member firms) and some of the advantages distinctive of the juridical autonomy of the group's member firms, such as the possibility of implementing efficient managerial incentive schemes. Second, in the light of the Japanese experience, a further important function performed by the industrial group is represented by the establishing of internal circuits of capital to allocate the available resources (see, e.g., Aoki, 1988). This mechanism (which will be more extensively analyzed in Chapter 8 below) may also be at work in the hierarchical group as shown by some recent empirical research (see, for the Italian case, Buzzacchi and Pagnini, 1994). Several other possible explanations have been put forward to justify the adoption of the group organizational form. For example, the takeover mechanism, commonly viewed as an integral aspect of the Anglo-American system of corporate governance, hardly operates in Japan. One role of interlocking shareholdings among firms may be to insulate management from external hostile takeover threats. This view is supported by the observation that interlocking shareholdings are typically associated with *stable shareholding arrangements*, i.e. agreements to hold the stock on a friendly basis. The interpretation of these arrangements is controversial. Some authors argue that they have contributed to the competitive strength of Japanese firms by enabling management to take a long term view of investments without being subject to short-term stock market pressures (Dore, 1986). Others identify them as a factor behind the alleged closedness of Japanese markets. (For a detailed analysis of the role of interlocking shareholdings in the Japanese system of corporate governance, see Sheard, 1994).

7.1.1 The Hierarchical Group

The hierarchical group has been described as a device either to limit the responsibilities of the controlling investor or to alter the degree of transparency of the actions taken in running the group's operations. Furthermore, more to the point of the present paper, the hierarchical group is a powerful mean of separating ownership and control (Berle and Means, 1933) and an effective way to allow the firm to grow whilst remaining under the control of an entrepreneur with limited resources. More specifically, the separation of ownership and control obtained through a pyramidal structure of power among (listed and non listed) firms allows the controlling investor to exercise power with a limited amount of capital (see the numerical example which concludes §7.2). In what follows we will mainly concentrate on the hierarchical business group, although the mathematical model developed in §7.2 is totally general. There is an inbuilt conflict of interests between the managers in control of a hierarchical business group (who act on behalf of the investor controlling the group and must therefore support global interests) and minority shareholders (who are only interested in the maximization of the value of the firm in which they have shares). This systematic conflict of interests between controlling investors and minority shareholders has been a continual source of concern in recent years for the securities exchange authorities of the countries of continental Europe. We hear everyday of changes in the ownership structure of business groups and yet we know very little of how minority shareholders are affected by such changes. In this paper we address the issue of the protection of minority shareholders in a business group. At present this is a particularly important issue in countries like, e.g., Italy where, as a result of a recent agreement between the Government and the Unions to change the state pension system, institutional investors (in particular, pension funds) are likely to channel a considerable proportion of their resources into financial markets in the near future. However, if institutional investors are ever to invest in the stock market, some protection of their interests must be guaranteed.

7.1.2 Overview of Part III

Part III of the book begins presenting in section 7.2 an analytical model developed by Brioschi et al. (1989, 1990, 1991) capable of describing the structure of ownership of large business groups. In particular, a mathematical description of the interdependence of value and ownership in a set of firms connected by cross-shareholding is reported. The framework presented in section 7.2 is extended in Chapter 8 and 9 to show how the hierarchical form of the business group may generate social inefficiencies in the process of allocation of resources within the firms belonging to the group. These inefficiencies stem from the conflict of interests between controlling investors and minority shareholders. In particular, in Chapter 8 we first set out a model which describes the functioning of a hierarchical group and then compare the structure of ownership and the investment allocation decisions in such a group with those of a multidivisional firm. Conditions are established on the integrated ownership of the group's controlling investor which make the latter preferable for minority shareholders. We also analyze how minority shareholders are affected by the way the group is managed and under rather general assumptions we derive precise relations between changes in the group's ownership structure and both the underlying and market values of the firms of the group. In Chapter 9 the links between ownership structure and investment decisions are analyzed using a quadratic approximation of firms' net profit functions.

Chapter 10 provides a brief overview of the general economic issues relating to institutional investors activity. Different regulatory frameworks are compared and the empirical experience accumulated in countries such U.K. and U.S. where institutional investors have significantly and persistently increased their holdings of equities is assessed.

In Chapter 11 the model developed in the previous Chapters is used to show how the problem of the defence of minority shareholders' interests in countries of Continental Europe like, e.g., Italy, could be at least partially alleviated, once institutional investors are allowed to grow and operate on the stock market, through an active involvement of institutions in firms' corporate governance. The intuition is very simple. To begin with, notice that even if Italian firms are generally characterized by strong concentration of ownership, nonetheless in a quarter of the largest quoted firms the control of the business group is only a minority control, i.e. control is collectively held by the firms belonging to the business group with a holding which altogether is a minority but large enough to dominate a shareholders' vote. This tendency toward a minority or *de facto* control seems to be inevitable if business groups want to take advantage of the large amount of liquidity provided by institutional investors. Consider now a large quoted firm belonging to a given business group where the control of the group is only de facto. This control "rests upon their ability to attract from scattered owners proxies sufficient when combined with their substantial minority interest to control the majority of the votes at the annual elections" (Bearle and Means, 1932). This presupposes there is no other grouping in an equally strong position: and this is exactly what happens today in Italy in a significant fraction of large quoted firms, with essentially non-existent institutional investors and the majority of the shares of large firms dispersed in small blocs. But once large fraction of the shares of the firm are in the hands of a few institutions, then the interests of these *large minority investors* (and therefore also the interests of all the remaining minority shareholders) will necessarily receive attention and consideration. Otherwise, if a firm is governed in the best interests of the holding group and not in the best interests of its own shareholders, institutional activism would be encouraged. In other words, if the management in place acts in the overall interests of the business group at the expense of the firm's shareholders (i.e. the inefficiencies described in Chapter 8 are too large) and institutions' interests are neglected in the managing of the firm by the business group, then a large investor may benefit from activism [36]. Thus, shareholder activism might be a response to the ownership generated inefficiencies in the internal allocation of the group's resources described in Chapter 8. We analyze in section 11.1 the incentives of a large institutional investor to make a proposal and we characterize the optimal amount of

---

[36] Notice that large investors who wishes to establish a reputation as tough shareholders might be ready to lose somehow in their business relations with one particular group in order to take advantage in their relations with another group. This issue is here not directly analyzed but the argument strengths the results of the analysis.

resources invested by proponents in soliciting support. In section 11.2, within the framework developed in Chapter 9, we then find the critical share that institutional investors should try to hold in order to receive positive net benefits from activism. Concluding remarks are provided in section 11.4.

7.2 Value and Ownership

In this section we will briefly review the mathematical model, originally developed by Brioschi, Buzzacchi and Colombo, 1989, 1990 and 1991, and then largely used in the literature (see, e.g., Ellerman, 1991, Fedenia, Hodder and Triantis, 1994, Baldone, Brioschi and Paleari, 1994), which will be used to define the concepts of value and ownership in a set of firms connected by cross-shareholdings. Extensive use will be made of a formal analogy with the equations describing a Leontiev-type linear economic model. A simple numerical example will conclude.

Consider a set of n firms quoted in a given stock market and connected through cross-shareholdings. In the following Chapters the n firms will be considered as constituting a hierarchical group, but as far as the analysis in this section is concerned, this assumption is not required. For the sake of simplicity, we will assume throughout the paper that the equity capital of the various firms is homogeneous (i.e. there is only one type of share). Let

$$A = [a_{lk}] \ , \quad l, k = 1, 2, \ldots, n$$

be the cross-shareholding matrix, i.e. a_{lk} is the share of the equity capital of firm k owned by firm l. Throughout the paper we will assume that the matrix A satisfy the following conditions:

i) for $l, k = 1, 2, \ldots, n$,

$$0 \leq a_{lk} \leq 1 \tag{7.1}$$

ii) for $k = 1, 2, \ldots, n$,

$$\sum_{l=1}^{n} a_{lk} \leq 1 \tag{7.2}$$

iii) the coefficients a_{lk} must be such as not to allow any subset composed of s firms ($s = 1, 2, \ldots, n$) to be entirely possessed by the s firms themselves.

Assumptions i) and ii) are obvious since a_{lk} is an ownership share. Assumptions iii) means that for every firm there must be a set of ultimate shareholders who are not firms. When these three assumptions are satisfied it is possible to show (see, e.g., Nikaido, 1970) that the largest eigenvalue (in absolute value) of matrix A, $\lambda(A)$ (the Frobenius root) satisfies

$$\lambda(A) < 1$$

and, moreover, $(I - A)$ has a non-negative inverse matrix $(I - A)^{-1}$. Furthermore, since $\lambda(A) = \lambda(A')$, $(I - A')$ also has a non-negative inverse matrix $(I - A')^{-1}$. These properties will be used extensively below.

In a market characterized by cross-shareholdings, for each listed firm j two measures of value are relevant. The first, denoted by v_j, is the (observable) market value of the equity of firm j and we will call it *the global value* of firm j. By definition, v_j is given by the product of the price of the share of firm j times the number of all issued shares. The second measure of value for firm j, denoted by w_j, is the (unobservable) value of firm j's own assets net of both the value of all holdings in firms belonging to the set considered and debt, also known as *the underlying value* of firm j. Notice that, while v_j is non-negative by definition, w_j may be either positive or negative (and in the latter case firm j is employing debt capital for financing its holdings in the other listed companies). Assuming linearity and additivity, the two measures of value are linked by the following Leontiev-type relation

$$v_j = w_j + \sum_{k=1}^{n} a_{jk} v_k \quad , \quad j = 1, 2, \ldots, n \tag{7.3}$$

Now let

$$w = \begin{pmatrix} w_1 \\ w_2 \\ \ldots \\ w_n \end{pmatrix} \quad , \quad v = \begin{pmatrix} v_1 \\ v_2 \\ \ldots \\ v_n \end{pmatrix}$$

so we can rewrite (7.3) in matrix terms as

$$v = w + Av \tag{7.4}$$

The assumptions stated above on matrix A guarantee that $(I-A)$ has a non -negative inverse matrix $(I-A)^{-1}$ so that we can solve (7.4) for vector v to obtain

$$v = (I - A)^{-1} w \tag{7.5}$$

Having described the model of values, we can now move on to the definitions of ownership that will be used throughout the paper. There are m investors in the economy. If x_{kl} is the share of firm l owned directly by investor k and $x_k = (x_{k1}, x_{k2}, \ldots, x_{kn})'$, then

$$X = \begin{pmatrix} x'_1 \\ x'_2 \\ \cdots \\ x'_m \end{pmatrix}$$

is the $(m \times n)$-matrix of the direct holdings of the m investors in the n firms. By definition, it follows that, for $j = 1, 2, \ldots, n$

$$\sum_{r=1}^{m} x_{rj} + \sum_{s=1}^{n} a_{sj} = 1 \tag{7.6}$$

Due to the presence of cross-shareholdings between the n firms, in addition to the direct ownership of investor k in firm l, it is also relevant to consider the indirect ownership of k in l, i.e. the fraction of l owned by k through the cross-shareholding matrix. We now define the *integrated ownership* of investor k in firm l, denoted by y_{kl}, as the sum of direct and indirect ownership of k in l, i.e.

$$y_{kl} = x_{kl} + \sum_{r=1}^{n} y_{kr} a_{rl} \ , \quad k, l = 1, 2, \ldots, n \tag{7.7}$$

If we now let $y_k = (y_{k1}, y_{k2}, \ldots, y_{kn})'$, then

$$Y = \begin{pmatrix} y'_1 \\ y'_2 \\ \cdots \\ y'_n \end{pmatrix}$$

is the $(m \times n)$-matrix of the integrated ownership of the m investors in the n firms.

In matrix terms (7.7) can be rewritten as

$$y_k = A'y_k + x_k \quad , \quad k = 1, 2, \ldots, n \qquad (7.7)'$$

which shows that integrated and direct ownership shares are also linked by a Leontiev-type relation. Again, given the assumptions on matrix A, we can solve for y_k to obtain

$$y_k = (I - A')^{-1} x_k \quad , \quad k = 1, 2, \ldots, n \qquad (7.8)$$

where (see above) also $(I - A')^{-1}$ is a non-negative matrix.

In terms of the above defined matrices X and Y, (7.7) can also be written as

$$Y = YA + X \qquad (7.7)''$$

so that (7.8) now becomes

$$Y = X(I - A)^{-1} \qquad (7.8)'$$

Notice that it is now easy to show that integrated ownership is complete, i.e. in each firm the integrated ownership of all investors add up to one. Indeed, if we rewrite equation (7.6) as

$$u'_m X + u'_n A = u'_n \qquad (7.9)$$

(where u_r is the r-vector of ones), i.e.

$$u'_m X(I - A)^{-1} = u'_n \quad , \qquad (7.9')$$

using (7.8)' we obtain

$$u'_m Y = u'_n \qquad (7.10)$$

and, finally,

$$\sum_{i=1}^{m} y_{ij} = 1 \ , \quad j = 1, 2, \ldots, n$$

i.e. the sum over investors of their integrated ownership in firm j is 1.

Let us now consider the vectors x_k and y_k of direct and integrated ownership of investor k. From (7.5) and (7.8) it follows that

$$x'_k v = y'_k w \qquad (7.11)$$

This equation allows us to identify the relation between value, ownership and property rights in a market characterized by cross-shareholdings: the direct holdings of an external investor can be seen as property rights on the global values of the given set of firms, while the integrated ownership represent property rights on the underlying values [37] (see, for details, Brioschi, Buzzacchi and Colombo, 1990, p.47-48).

As explained in §7.1.1, the hierarchical group is a powerful device to separate ownership and control and an effective way for an investor (or a coalition of investors) with limited resources to gain control cheaply over a larger number of assets than would otherwise be possible. The share of residual claims on a group's assets held by the controlling investor may be rather limited. A simple example may be useful to clarify the point (and illustrate the models of value and ownership presented above). Consider a pyramidal group composed of two firms. Firm 1 is a parent holding company having no assets except a 60% shareholding in firm 2 which is an operating subsidiary where all the group's assets are concentrated, i.e.

FIRM 1

0.6

FIRM 2

---

[37] Equation (7.11) can also be derived simply noticing that the two systems of equations defining value and ownership are formally identical to the primal and dual system in the Leontiev model, (see Nikaido, 1970.)

In terms of the notation introduced above we have

$$A = \begin{pmatrix} 0 & .6 \\ 0 & 0 \end{pmatrix} \quad , \quad w = \begin{pmatrix} 0 \\ 100 \end{pmatrix}$$

Both firms are listed. The controlling investor (investor 1) directly holds 60% of the shares of the holding company but has no direct shareholding in the subsidiary. The second investor is intended to represent the market. In terms of the notation of this chapter,

$$x_1 = \begin{pmatrix} .6 \\ 0 \end{pmatrix} \quad , \quad x_2 = \begin{pmatrix} .4 \\ .4 \end{pmatrix}$$

and so

$$X = \begin{pmatrix} .6 & 0 \\ .4 & .4 \end{pmatrix}$$

Solving (7.4) and (7.7)' we obtain

$$v = \begin{pmatrix} 60 \\ 100 \end{pmatrix} \quad , \quad y_1 = \begin{pmatrix} .6 \\ .36 \end{pmatrix} \quad , \quad y_2 = \begin{pmatrix} .4 \\ .64 \end{pmatrix}$$

and so

$$Y = \begin{pmatrix} .6 & .36 \\ .4 & .64 \end{pmatrix} \tag{7.12}$$

Thus despite the fact that outside stockholders hold the majority (64%) of the residual claims on the group's assets, they are deprived of control [38]. Lacking control over the assets on which they hold the majority of residual claims, the group member firms minority shareholders are exposed to the threat of expropriation of wealth on the part of the group's controlling investor. This issue is addressed in the next Chapters.

---

[38] More generally (see Brioschi et al., 1990), in a strictly pyramidal group composed of N firms, the share of residual claims on group assets held by the controlling investor may be as low as $(.5 + \epsilon)^N$ without any threat of losing control. Such share may be much lower (equal to $(.25 + \epsilon)^N$) if, as allowed by the Italian law, non-voting stock accounts for half of the equity capital of the N firms.

Chapter 8

Corporate Grouping and Resource Allocation

8.1 Resource Allocation in a Group

This Chapter is devoted to analyze how resources are allocated among member firms in a hierarchical business group. Investment decisions taken within this organizational structure will be compared with those taken within the classical multidivisional firm. The above issues will be addressed from the perspective of minority (or non controlling) shareholders, that is it will be investigated how the latter are affected by the group's organizational structure.

We build on recent work by Buzzacchi and Pagnini (1995). In their paper, Buzzacchi and Pagnini show how the organizational form of a hierarchical business group may itself be responsible for generating inefficiencies in the allocation of resources. These inefficiencies stem from the conflicts of interests between the investor controlling the whole group and the shareholders of a single firm belonging to the group. In this chapter we extend their analysis in several directions. First, in order to analyze how business group minority shareholders are affected by the way the group is managed, we set out a model which describes how resources are allocated in a corporate group. We then compare the group form with the multidivisional firm, and establish conditions on the integrated ownership of the group's controlling investor which make the multidivision preferable for minority shareholders. Furthermore, we investigate how the group's ownership structure affects the value of the shareholdings of outside investors. This is an important issue in assessing the likely impact of the entry of institutional investors (usually not involved in control and instead rather passive shareholders) in markets (like, e.g., the Italian one) characterized by the massive presence of business groups. We analyze how the single group's member firms are affected by the way the group is managed. In particular, we derive, under rather general assumptions, precise relations between the group's trading activity in the stock market and both the underlying and market values of the firms of the group. The analysis here developed aims at providing a minimal framework to establish how institutional investors such as pension funds should behave once allowed to invest in the equity market in order to protect their beneficiaries. This issue is the subject of Chapter 11 below.

We will make use of the mathematical model presented in section 7.2; in particular, the two sets of equations linking integrated and direct ownership and market and underlying values will be extensively used. Let us consider a business group, consisting of n firms linked through the $n \times n$-matrix A of cross-shareholdings, and a set of m investors. As in §7.2, let X and Y be the $m \times n$-matrices of direct and integrated ownership, and let v and w the n-vectors of market and underlying values. In running the business operations of the group several decisions need to be taken: we will focus on the task of allocating the available capital among the n firms belonging to the group. In a hierarchical business group the allocation of capital may be considered as a decision autonomously taken by the controlling investor/shareholder (investor i in what follows) who is here assumed to simply maximize the value of his portfolio. If x_{ij} and y_{ij} are, respectively, the direct and integrated ownership of investor i in firm j $(j = 1, 2, \ldots, n)$, then the value, at market prices, of the portfolio of the controlling shareholder is given by

$$p = \sum_{j=1}^{n} x_{ij} v_j$$

and, from (7.11), it follows immediately that this value can also be expressed in terms of integrated ownership as

$$p = \sum_{j=1}^{n} y_{ij} w_j$$

The constrained maximization problem faced by the controlling investor is therefore

$$\max_{\phi_1,\ldots,\phi_n} \sum_{j=1}^{n} y_{ij}\, w_j(\phi_j)$$

$$\text{s.t.} \quad \sum_{j=1}^{n} \phi_j \leq M$$

(8.1)

where ϕ_j is the amount of capital to be allocated to firm j, $M > 0$ can be thought of as the total cash flow of the group's member firms, and if an amount of capital ϕ_j is allocated to firm j, then $w_j(\phi_j)$ is the corresponding underlying value of firm j. The formalization here proposed neglects the private benefits accruing to the controlling investor from his being in charge of the group. A more general setting should take into consideration also other motives in explaining within group capital allocation. Our analysis, however, is intended as a first step toward such a more complete framework.

To make the analysis interesting we will assume that the business group is capital constrained, that is the constraint in problem (8.1) is binding and so the corresponding Lagrange multiplier is positive. As shown by Buzzacchi and Pagnini (1995), if the w_js are differentiable, with $w_j'(\phi_j) > 0$ and $w_j''(\phi_j) < 0$, it follows that (8.1) has a solution satisfying

$$y_{ij_1}\, w_{j_1}'(\phi_{j_1}) = y_{ij_2}\, w_{j_2}'(\phi_{j_2}) \quad , \quad j_1, j_2 = 1, 2, \ldots, n$$

with a distortion in the allocation of resources caused by the weights (the integrated ownership of the controlling investor) in the constrained maximization (8.1). However, it is not clear whether minority shareholders lose or gain from investing in a particular firm belonging to the group and, more generally, it would be interesting to establish the conditions (if any) which might make the hierarchical grouping desirable for non controlling investors. To answer the above questions, however, a comparison with some *feasible* alternative allocation is required.

In order to determine the properties of the solution of the constrained maximization problem (8.1) note, first, that once i, the identity of the controlling investor, is fixed the cross-shareholdings matrix, A, and the i-th row, x'_i, of the direct holdings matrix X uniquely determine through (7.7) the weights y_{ij} in the objective function of (8.1). If the available capital, M, has also been fixed, we are left with the task of specifying the value functions w_js. Let

$$w_j(\phi_j) = f_j(\phi_j) - r\phi_j \quad , \quad j = 1, 2, \ldots, n \qquad (8.2)$$

where f_j is the profit function of firm j and r is the internal opportunity cost of funds. Thus, w_j is firm j's profit net of the opportunity cost of capital. We assume that, for each $j = 1, 2, \ldots, n$, f_j is twice differentiable with respect to the allocated amount of capital, and the following conditions are satisfied:

i) $f_j(0) \geq 0$,

ii) $f'_j(\phi_j) > 0$ for $\phi_j \geq 0$, and

$$\lim_{\phi_j \to 0+} f'_j(\phi_j) = +\infty \quad ,$$

iii) $f''_j(\phi_j) < 0$ for $\phi_j \geq 0$.

This framework seems sufficiently general for the purpose of this Chapter. We defer to the next Chapter for the analysis of a quadratic approximation of (8.2).

Without loss of generality we can assume that $y_{ij} > 0$, $j = 1, 2, \ldots, n$ [39]. The first order conditions for a maximum when (8.2) holds may be stated as

$$y_{ij}\left(f'_j(\phi_j) - r\right) = \lambda \quad , \quad j = 1, 2, \ldots, n \qquad (8.3)$$

and

$$\sum_{j=1}^{n} \phi_j = M \qquad (8.4)$$

---

[39] If, for some $j = j^*$, $y_{ij^*} = 0$, the controlling investor does not allocate any resource to firm j^*.

Conditions i), ii) and iii) guarantee that problem (8.1) has a unique and positive solution, which we will denote by $\tilde{\phi}_j^i(A, x_i, M)$ $(j = 1, 2, \ldots n)$ and $\lambda(A, x_i, M)$, for given values of the parameters A, x_i and M. Moreover, the solution of (8.3) and (8.4) completely characterizes the optimum. Since the constraint is binding (and so $\lambda > 0$), from (8.3) it follows immediately that the amount of resources allocated to each firm depends on the integrated ownership of the controlling investor in that firm. In particular, at the optimum, the marginal productivity of capital will be higher in firms with low controlling investor's integrated ownership. Correspondingly, because f_j' is strictly decreasing, such firms will have less capital than they could otherwise have obtained.

We now investigate the conditions under which non controlling shareholders suffer a loss from their firm being part of a business group. In order to do this we have to consider an alternative organizational structure for the n production activities $w_1, w_2, \ldots, w_n$. Let us assume that in the constrained maximization problem (8.1) the weights of the objective function satisfy, for each $j = 1, 2, \ldots, n$, the condition

$$y_{ij} = y_i > 0 \tag{8.5}$$

This is tantamount to assuming that the investor-decision making has the same (integrated) ownership in each firm of the group, and therefore the above condition corresponds to the allocation of capital to the different divisions of a unique large firm (the so called *multidivisional firm*). In this case the first order conditions of problem (8.1) become

$$(f_j'(\phi_j) - r) = \mu/y_i \quad , \quad j = 1, 2, \ldots, n \tag{8.6}$$

and (8.4) also holds. Let $\tilde{\tilde{\phi}}_j(A, x_i, M)$, $j = 1, 2, \ldots, n$, be the solution of (8.1) when (8.5) is satisfied. Notice that now the amount of capital allocated to firm j is independent of the identity of the investor-decision making, i.e. it is now totally irrelevant who is in charge of allocating the capital to the different production units. This is in complete contrast with the case of the business

group previously analyzed since, from (8.3), the group's ownership structure directly affects the amount of resources available
for each firm in the group. In order to assess which organizational
form is preferable for the shareholders of the generic firm (or division) j, we must compare the amounts of resources allocated
to j by the two different forms of ownership structure (each with
the corresponding corporate governance model). Comparing (8.3)
and (8.6), since f'_j is a strictly decreasing function, we have that,
for each $j = 1, 2, \ldots, n$, $\tilde{\tilde{\phi}}_j > \tilde{\phi}^i_j$ if and only if

$$\frac{\mu}{y_i} < \frac{\lambda}{y_{ij}}$$

i.e.

$$y_{ij} < y^*_i \tag{8.7}$$

where

$$y^*_i = \left(\frac{\lambda}{\mu}\right) y_i \tag{8.8}$$

When (8.7) is satisfied, i.e. when the integrated ownership in
firm j of the controlling investor is lower than the critical value
y^*_i, the multidivisional form is preferable for firm j shareholders.
Conversely, they prefer the group form when $y_{ij} > y^*_i$. The intuition for this result is simple. In the multidivisional firm marginal
productivities of capital are equated across firms and capital allocated accordingly. The hierarchical grouping form modifies this
simple efficient rule by equating across firms the marginal productivities of capital each multiplied by the corresponding integrated
ownership of the controlling investor. In firms with low controlling investor's integrated ownership the marginal productivity of
capital will therefore be high, and the capital low.

Now, let us introduce the optimal value function of the constrained maximization problem (8.1), defined as

$$V^i_G(A, x_i, M) \equiv \sum_{j=1}^{n} y_{ij}(A, x_i)(f_j(\tilde{\phi}^i_j) - r\tilde{\phi}^i_j)$$

Then, by the envelope theorem, when V_G^i is differentiable, we have

$$\partial V_G^i / \partial M = \lambda(A, x_i, M) \tag{8.9}$$

Thus the Lagrange multiplier signifies the marginal rate of change of the maximum value function V_G^i with respect to a change in the available total capital, i.e. the shadow price of capital. Similarly for the multidivisional firm, if

$$V_{MD}(M, y_i) \equiv \sum_{j=1}^{n} y_i \left(f_j(\tilde{\phi}_j) - r\tilde{\phi}_j \right) \tag{8.10}$$

we also have

$$\partial V_{MD} / \partial M = \mu(M) \tag{8.11}$$

Since $V_{MD}(M, y_i) = y_i V_{MD}(M, 1)$, we can conclude that

$$y_i^* = \frac{\partial V_G^i(A, x_i, M) / \partial M}{\partial V_{MD}(M, 1) / \partial M} \tag{8.12}$$

Thus the critical integrated ownership in (8.8) is the ratio of the shadow prices of capital in the business group and in the fully owned multi-divisional.

We summarize in the following Proposition the results derived in the above analysis.

PROPOSITION 8.1

Consider a capital constrained hierarchical business group, consisting of n firms, and a particular firm belonging to the group (say, firm j). Then, the amount of capital allocated to firm j is an increasing function of y_{ij} (the integrated ownership of the controlling investor in firm j). Moreover, if we limit the analysis only to comparisons of the group and the multidivisional organizational structures, the shareholders of firm j are suffering a loss from their firm being part of the business group if and only if (8.7) holds.

8.2 Ownership Structure and Value

Let us now return to the analysis of firm j as part of the business group. In particular, we want to investigate how the group's ownership structure affects both the amount of resources allocated to and the underlying value of each firm in the group. As shown in §7.2, the group's ownership structure is characterized by the vector $y_i = (y_{i1}, y_{i2}, \ldots, y_{in})'$ of the controlling investor's integrated ownership. Moreover, from eq.(7.8), we know that

$$y_i = (I - A')^{-1} x_i \qquad (8.13)$$

where $x_i = (x_{i1}, x_{i2}, \ldots, x_{in})'$ is the vector of the controlling investor's direct holdings, and A is the cross-shareholding matrix. From (8.13) it follows that, in order to analyze the effect of the ownership structure on the amount of resources allocated (and, correspondigly, on the underlying and global values), we need to investigate how $\tilde{\phi}_j^i$ is going to be affected by $a)$ a change in the vector x_i of i's direct holdings, and $b)$ a change in the cross-shareholding matrix A. Let us first focus on $a)$ and, in particular, let us analyze how the available amount of resources allocated to firm j ($j = 1, 2, \ldots, n$) is affected by an increase in the controlling investor's direct holding in firm k (obtained through a purchasing of firm k shares from the market, i.e. from individual investors or firms not belonging to the group). Parametrically differentiating (8.3) and (8.4) with respect to x_{ik}, $k = 1, 2, \ldots, n$, we obtain

$$y_{ij} f_j''(\phi_j) \frac{\partial \tilde{\phi}_j^i}{x_{ik}} - \frac{\partial \lambda}{\partial x_{ik}} + b_{kj} \left(f_j'(\phi_j) - r \right) = 0 \quad , \quad j = 1, 2, \ldots, n$$
$$(8.14)$$

and

$$\sum_{s=1}^{n} \frac{\partial \tilde{\phi}_s^i}{\partial x_{ik}} = 0 \qquad (8.15)$$

where we have indicated the elements of the matrix $B = (I - A)^{-1}$ by b_{lm}. Now, (8.14) and (8.15) are a linear system of $(n+1)$ equations in $(n+1)$ unknowns (the n partial derivatives, $\partial \tilde{\phi}_j^i / x_{ik}$, and the partial derivative of the Lagrange multiplier, $\partial \lambda / \partial x_{ik}$). Assumption iii) above now guarantees that this system has a unique solution [40]. Dividing (8.14) by $y_{ij} f_j''(\phi_j)$, summing over j, and using (8.15), implies that

$$\frac{\partial \lambda}{\partial x_{ik}} = \frac{1}{z_0} \sum_{s=1}^{n} \frac{b_{ks}(f_s' - r)}{y_{is} f_s''} \tag{8.16}$$

where $f_j'' \equiv f_j''(\tilde{\phi}_j^i)$, $j = 1, 2, \ldots, n$, and

$$z_0 \equiv \sum_{h=1}^{n} \frac{1}{y_{ih} f_h''} \tag{8.17}$$

Moreover, directly from (8.14), we also obtain

$$\frac{\partial \tilde{\phi}_j^i}{\partial x_{ik}} = \frac{1}{y_{ij} f_j''} \left[\frac{\partial \lambda}{\partial x_{ik}} - b_{kj}(f_j' - r) \right] \quad , \quad j = 1, 2, \ldots, n \tag{8.18}$$

Let us now consider how $\tilde{\phi}_j^i$ $(j = 1, 2, \ldots, n)$ is affected by an increase in the fraction a_{lk} of firm k owned by firm l (obtained through a purchasing of firm k shares by firm l from the market).

---

[40] The matrix of the coefficients, M, is given by

$$M = \begin{pmatrix} \Delta & -u \\ u' & 0 \end{pmatrix}$$

where

$$\Delta = \begin{pmatrix} y_{i1} f_1'' & 0 & \cdots & 0 \\ 0 & y_{i2} f_2'' & \cdots & 0 \\ \cdots & \cdots & \cdots & \cdots \\ 0 & 0 & \cdots & y_{in} f_n'' \end{pmatrix} \quad , \quad u = \begin{pmatrix} 1 \\ \vdots \\ 1 \end{pmatrix}$$

and therefore

$$|M| = (u' \Delta^{-1} u)|\Delta| \neq 0$$

Parametrically differentiating (8.3) and (8.4) with respect to a_{lk}, the same argument as above now implies that for $l, k = 1, 2, \ldots, n$,

$$\frac{\partial \lambda}{\partial a_{lk}} = y_{il} \frac{\partial \lambda}{\partial x_{ik}} \tag{8.19}$$

and

$$\frac{\partial \tilde{\phi}_j^i}{\partial a_{lk}} = y_{il} \frac{\partial \tilde{\phi}_j^i}{\partial x_{ik}} \quad , \quad j = 1, 2, \ldots, n \tag{8.20}$$

Finally, let us consider how the two above described changes in the group's ownership structure affect the actual underlying value of firm j. Since

$$\frac{\partial w_j}{\partial x_{ik}}(\tilde{\phi}_j^i) = \frac{\partial w_j}{\partial \phi_j}(\tilde{\phi}_j^i) \frac{\partial \tilde{\phi}_j^i}{\partial x_{ik}} \quad , \quad j = 1, 2, \ldots, n \tag{8.21}$$

and for $l = 1, 2, \ldots, n$

$$\frac{\partial w_j}{\partial a_{lk}}(\tilde{\phi}_j^i) = \frac{\partial w_j}{\partial \phi_j}(\tilde{\phi}_j^i) \frac{\partial \tilde{\phi}_j^i}{\partial a_{lk}} \quad , \quad j = 1, 2, \ldots, n \tag{8.22}$$

from the assumptions on the w_js it follows immediately that to analyze how changes in x_{ik} and a_{lk} $(j, l = 1, 2, \ldots, n)$ affect the underlying value of firm j all we need to know is how these changes affect the amount of resources allocated to firm j.

We can now prove the following Proposition:

PROPOSITION 8.2

Consider a capital constrained hierarchical business group, consisting of n firms, and a particular firm belonging to the group (say, firm k). Then, an increase in the controlling investor's direct holding in firm k (obtained through a purchasing of firm k shares from the market, i.e. from individual investors or firms not belonging to the group) will raise both the amount of resources allocated to firm k and (consequently) the realized underlying value of firm k. Moreover, an increase in the fraction a_{lk} of firm k owned by firm l (obtained through a purchasing of firm k shares by firm l

from the market) will also increase both the resources allocated to firm k and (consequently) the realized underlying value of firm k.

Proof: see Appendix.

From (8.20), (8.21) and (8.22) it follows immediately that

$$\frac{\partial w_j^i}{\partial a_{lk}}(\tilde{\phi}_j^i) = y_{il}\frac{\partial w_j^i}{\partial x_{ik}}(\tilde{\phi}_j^i) \qquad (8.23)$$

so that, setting $j = k$ in (8.23) and recalling that $y_{il} \in (0,1)$, $l = 1, 2, \ldots, n$, we have the following Corollary:

COROLLARY

Consider a capital constrained hierarchical business group, consisting of n firms, and two particular firms belonging to the group (say, firm j and firm l). Then the effect on $w_j^i(\tilde{\phi}_j^i)$ of a purchasing of firm j shares by firm l from the market is proportional to the effect of a purchasing of firm j shares by the controlling investor, the coefficient of proportionality being the integrated ownership of the controlling investor in firm l. Also, the latter effect is larger than the former.

As mentioned in §7.2, in a market characterized by cross-shareholdings among firms two measures of value can be defined, i.e. underlying and market values. However, the analysis developed so far has only considered the effects of the group's investment strategies on the underlying values of the various firms belonging to the group, and the effects on market values have not yet been considered. Underlying values are difficult to observe but provide more truthful information on firms' financial wealth, whereas market values are easily observed (if the firm is listed) but can easily be inflated trough the exchange of shares among firms belonging to the same group.

Let (to simplify notations)

$$\tilde{w}_j^i \equiv w_j(\tilde{\phi}_j^i) \tag{8.24}$$

and

$$\tilde{w}^i \equiv (\tilde{w}_1^i, \tilde{w}_2^i, \ldots, \tilde{w}_n^i)' \tag{8.25}$$

As we know from equations (7.3) and (7.4), the two measures of value are linked through a Leontiev type relation, so that when underlying values are given by (8.25), then the corresponding market values, for $j = 1, 2, \ldots, n$, are

$$\tilde{v}_j^i \equiv \left(B\tilde{w}^i \right)_j$$

$$= \sum_{s=1}^{n} b_{js} \left(f_s(\tilde{\phi}_s^i) - r\tilde{\phi}_s^i \right) \tag{8.26}$$

where (see above) $B = (I - A)^{-1}$. The same results derived with reference to underlying values can now also be obtained for market values. Indeed, deriving eq.(8.26) with respect to x_{ik} and a_{lk} ($l, k = 1, 2, \ldots n$), after some simple algebra, we obtain

$$\frac{\partial \tilde{v}_j^i}{\partial x_{ik}} = \sum_{s=1}^{n} b_{js} \frac{\partial \tilde{\phi}_s^i}{\partial x_{ik}} (f_s'(\tilde{\phi}_s^i) - r) \quad , \quad j = 1, 2, \ldots, n \tag{8.27}$$

and

$$\frac{\partial \tilde{v}_j^i}{\partial a_{lk}} = b_{jl} \tilde{v}_k^i + y_{il} \frac{\partial \tilde{v}_j^i}{\partial x_{ik}} \quad , \quad j = 1, 2, \ldots, n \tag{8.28}$$

so that, setting $j = k$ in(8.27) and (8.28) we obtain

$$\frac{\partial \tilde{v}_k^i}{\partial x_{ik}} = \sum_{s=1}^{n} b_{ks} \frac{\partial \tilde{\phi}_s^i}{\partial x_{ik}} (f_s'(\tilde{\phi}_s^i - r) \quad , \quad k = 1, 2, \ldots, n \tag{8.27}'$$

and

$$\frac{\partial \tilde{v}_k^i}{\partial a_{lk}} = b_{kl} \tilde{v}_k^i + y_{il} \frac{\partial \tilde{v}_k^i}{\partial x_{ik}} \quad , \quad k = 1, 2, \ldots, n \tag{8.28}'$$

We can now prove the following Proposition:

PROPOSITION 8.3

Consider a capital constrained hierarchical business group, consisting of n firms, and a particular firm belonging to the group (say, firm k). Then

i) an increase in the controlling investor's direct holding in firm k (obtained through a purchasing of firm k shares from the market) will raise the realized market value of firm k, (i.e. also the market value of each firm is a strictly increasing function of the controlling investor's direct holding in that firm);

ii) an increase in the fraction a_{lk} of firm k owned by firm l (obtained through a purchasing of firm k shares by firm l from the market) will also increase the realized market value of firm k.

Proof: see Appendix.

Let us now summarize the findings of the model presented in this section. In a hierarchical business group the available resources (say, capital for investments) are allocated to member firms through a centralized process which strongly depends on the group's ownership structure. In particular, the amount of resources allocated to any given firm (say, firm j) by the controlling investor is an increasing function of his integrated ownership in that firm. Comparing the group and the multidivisional forms, we have also shown that, from the perspective of each group's firm non controlling shareholders, only when the controlling investor's integrated ownership in that firm is sufficiently high is the group's structure the more preferable arrangement. Conversely, in firms with low controlling investor's integrated ownership minority shareholders suffer a loss from their firm being part of the group, and the multidivisional form would be more profitable. We have also investigate how both changes in the cross-shareholding matrix and in the controlling investor's vector of direct holdings affect resources, underlying values, and market values of the group's member firms. We have shown that, for each firm, these functions all increase in correspondence to both an increase in the controlling investor's direct holding and an increase in any other member firm's holdings in that firm.

In sum, the above analysis seems to provide a simple analytical framework to investigate how the decisions of groups' controlling investors affect the investment of non controlling investors. It is worth emphasize that where the corporate form of grouping is predominant, equity markets tend to be poorly developed and minority shareholders' rights are not an issue. These characteristics are reflected in the large power that controlling investors have to affect non controlling shareholders. In this perspective, a proper understanding of business groups' internal functioning seem to be an essential preliminary step in order to develop an appropriate legal and regulatory framework capable to enhance the importance of equity market and at the same time limit the excessive power of a few large investors.

Appendix

Proof of Propositions 8.2 and 8.3

Proof of Proposition 8.2

We will first prove that $\tilde{\phi}_k^i$ is strictly increasing with x_{ik}. From (8.16) and (8.17), given the assumptions on f_j, it follows immediately that $\partial\lambda/\partial x_{ik} > 0$. Moreover, from (8.18) $\partial\tilde{\phi}_j^i/\partial x_{ik} > 0$ if and only if

$$\frac{\partial\lambda}{\partial x_{ik}} < b_{kj}\left(f_j' - r\right) \qquad (A8.1)$$

In particular, setting $j = k$, we have that $\partial\tilde{\phi}_k^i/\partial x_{ik}$ is positive iff

$$\left(\frac{1}{z_0}\right)\sum_{s=1}^{n}\frac{b_{ks}\left(f_s' - r\right)}{y_{is}\,f_s''} < b_{kk}\left(f_k' - r\right) \qquad (A8.2)$$

which simplifies to

$$\sum_{s=1}^{n}\frac{1}{y_{is}\,f_s''}\left[b_{ks}\left(f_s' - r\right) - b_{kk}\left(f_k' - r\right)\right] > 0 \qquad (A8.3)$$

A sufficient condition for (A8.3) to hold is that, for each $s = 1, 2, \ldots, n$

$$b_{ks}\left(f_s' - r\right) < b_{kk}\left(f_k' - r\right) \qquad (A8.4)$$

that is (using the first order conditions)

$$\frac{b_{ks}}{y_{is}} < \frac{b_{kk}}{y_{ik}} \qquad (A8.5)$$

Now, from (7.8), we have

$$y_{il} = \sum_{r=1}^{n} b_{rl}\,x_{ir}$$

so that (A8.5) becomes

$$\frac{1}{b_{kk}} \Big(\sum_{r=1}^{n} b_{rk} x_{ir} \Big) < \frac{1}{b_{ks}} \Big(\sum_{r=1}^{n} b_{rs} x_{ir} \Big) \qquad (A8.6)$$

i.e.

$$\sum_{r=1}^{n} x_{ir} \Big(\frac{b_{rk}}{b_{kk}} - \frac{b_{rs}}{b_{ks}} \Big) < 0 \qquad (A8.7)$$

Since $x_{ir} \in (0,1)$ $\forall r = 1, 2, \ldots, n$, a sufficient condition for (8.25) to hold is that

$$\frac{b_{rk}}{b_{kk}} < \frac{b_{rs}}{b_{ks}} \ , \ \forall r, k, s = 1, 2, \ldots, n \ , \ r \neq k \neq s \qquad (A8.8)$$

which is a particular case of Theorem 16, p.120, in Murata (1977). We have so proved that

$$\frac{\partial \tilde{\phi}_k^i}{\partial x_{ik}} > 0 \ , \quad k = 1, 2, \ldots, n \qquad (A8.9)$$

From (A8.9) and (8.20) it now follows immediately that, for $l = 1, 2, \ldots, n$

$$\frac{\partial \tilde{\phi}_k^i}{a_{lk}} > 0 \ , \quad k = 1, 2, \ldots, n \qquad (A8.10)$$

Let us, finally, consider how changes in the group's ownership structure affect the underlying value of firm j. Setting $j = k$ in (8.21) and (8.22), from the first order conditions and from (A8.9) and (A8.10) we immediately have

$$\frac{\partial w_k}{\partial x_{ik}} (\tilde{\phi}_k^i) = \frac{\partial w_k}{\partial \phi_k} (\tilde{\phi}_k^i) \frac{\partial \tilde{\phi}_k^i}{\partial x_{ik}} > 0 \ , \quad k = 1, 2, \ldots, n \qquad (A8.11)$$

and for $l = 1, 2, \ldots, n$

$$\frac{\partial w_k}{\partial a_{lk}} (\tilde{\phi}_k^i) = \frac{\partial w_k}{\partial \phi_k} (\tilde{\phi}_k^i) \frac{\partial \tilde{\phi}_k^i}{\partial a_{lk}} > 0 \ , \quad k = 1, 2, \ldots, n \qquad (A8.12)$$

which completes the proof.

Proof of Proposition 8.3

Let us first prove i). From (8.27)', (8.18) and (8.16), and using the first order conditions (8.3), it follows that to prove that $\tilde{v}_k^i$ is strictly increasing with x_{ik} is tantamount to prove that

$$\sum_{s=1}^{n} \frac{b_{ks}}{y_{is}^2 f_s''} \left[\frac{1}{z_0} \sum_{t=1}^{n} \frac{b_{kt}(f_t' - r)}{y_{it} f_t''} - b_{ks}(f_s' - r) \right] > 0 \qquad (A8.13)$$

Using (8.17), the above condition becomes

$$\sum_{s=1}^{n} \frac{b_{ks}}{y_{is}^2 f_s''} \left[\sum_{t=1}^{n} \frac{b_{kt}(f_t' - r) - b_{ks}(f_s' - r)}{y_{it} f_t''} \right] < 0 \qquad (A8.14)$$

i.e.

$$\sum_{s,t=1}^{n} \frac{b_{ks}}{y_{is}^2 f_s'' y_{it} f_t''} \left(\frac{b_{kt}}{y_{it}} - \frac{b_{ks}}{y_{is}} \right) < 0 \qquad (A8.15)$$

Define (for $t, s = 1, 2, \ldots, n$)

$$Q_{ts} = \frac{b_{kt}}{y_{it}} - \frac{b_{ks}}{y_{is}}$$

$$P_{ts} = \frac{1}{f_t'' f_s''} \frac{1}{y_{it} y_{is}} Q_{ts}$$

and

$$R_{ik} = \sum_{t,s=1}^{n} \frac{b_{ks}}{y_{is}} P_{ts} \qquad (A8.16)$$

so that (A8.15) becomes

$$R_{ik} < 0 \qquad (A8.17)$$

Since

$$Q_{st} = -Q_{ts}$$

we also have

$$P_{st} = -P_{ts}$$

From the definition of R_{ik} in (A8.16), switching indexes, we obtain

$$R_{ik} = \sum_{s,t=1}^{n} \frac{b_{kt}}{y_{it}} P_{st} = - \sum_{s,t=1}^{n} \frac{b_{kt}}{y_{it}} P_{ts} \qquad (A8.18)$$

and adding together (A8.16) and (A8.18) we finally have

$$2R_{ik} = \sum_{t,s=1}^{n} P_{ts} \left(\frac{b_{ks}}{y_{is}} - \frac{b_{kt}}{y_{it}} \right)$$

$$= - \sum_{t,s=1}^{n} P_{ts} Q_{ts}$$

$$= - \sum_{t,s=1}^{n} \frac{1}{f_t''} \frac{1}{f_s''} \frac{1}{y_{it}} \frac{1}{y_{is}} Q_{ts}^2 < 0$$

so that (A8.17) holds true and i) is proved. Part ii) now follows immediately by inspection of (8.28)'.

Chapter 9

Ownership and Investments:
A Numerical Example

This Chapter is devoted to the analysis of a numerical example. In Chapter 8 above we compared the structure of ownership and corporate governance in a group with those of a multidivisional firm and we established, in a rather general framework, conditions on the integrated ownership of the group's controlling investor which make the multidivision preferable for minority shareholders (see Proposition 8.1). We also derived some comparative static results concerning how changes in the group's ownership structure affect resources and values in member firms (see Proposition 8.2). In this appendix we will take a quadratic approximation of the value function (8.2) and we will repeat the analysis developed in the preceeding Chapter. The advantage of this approach is that, under a quadratic approximization, is possible to obtain a closed form solution of the constrained maximization problem (8.1), so that the influence of ownership structure on corporate investment decisions can be directly analyzed.

Let the function describing the underlying value of the generic firm of the group (see eq.(8.2))

$$w_j(\phi_j) = -\gamma_j(\phi_j - \bar{\phi}_j)^2 + \gamma_j\bar{\phi}_j^2 \qquad (9.1)$$

where γ_j and $\bar{\phi}_j$ are positive constants. This particular functional form is tantamount to assume that each firm is characterized by an optimal allocation of capital, i.e. for each firm j there is an amount of capital $\bar{\phi}_j > 0$ which would maximize the value w_j of firm j alone. Also, the parameter γ_j can be interpreted as a measure of firm j's productivity (high values of γ_j being associated with high productivity of capital for firm j). As in Chapter 8, we will assume that the business group is capital constrained, i.e. the constraint in problem (8.1) is binding [41] and so

$$\sum_{j=1}^{n} \bar{\phi}_j > M$$

We will also assume that, for $j = 1, 2, \ldots, n$,

$$\bar{\phi}_j \leq M$$

so that the available capital would be sufficient to maximize the value of firm j alone.

Using equation (9.1) and letting

$$\phi = \begin{pmatrix} \phi_1 \\ \phi_2 \\ \ldots \\ \phi_n \end{pmatrix}, \quad \bar{\phi} = \begin{pmatrix} \bar{\phi}_1 \\ \bar{\phi}_2 \\ \ldots \\ \bar{\phi}_n \end{pmatrix}$$

problem (8.1) becomes

$$\max_{\phi} \ -(\phi - \bar{\phi})' \Delta (\phi - \bar{\phi}) + K \tag{A2}$$

$$\text{s.t.} \quad u'\phi \leq M$$

where $u' = (1, \ldots, 1)$ and

$$\Delta = \begin{pmatrix} \gamma_1 y_{i1} & 0 & \cdots & 0 \\ 0 & \gamma_2 y_{i2} & \cdots & 0 \\ \ldots & \ldots & \ldots & \ldots \\ 0 & 0 & \cdots & \gamma_n y_{in} \end{pmatrix}, \quad K = \sum_{j=1}^{n} \gamma_j \bar{\phi}_j^2$$

---

[41] Otherwise the solution of problem (8.1) would simply be $\phi_j = \bar{\phi}_j$, $j = 1, 2, \ldots, n$, and the shareholders of firm j would not suffer any loss.

The solution to problem (9.2), i.e. the allocation of the available capital to the n firms belonging to the business group when the i-th investor is in control, denoted by $\tilde{\phi}^i$, is given by

$$\tilde{\phi}^i = \bar{\phi} - \frac{s}{\eta_i} \begin{pmatrix} 1/\gamma_1 y_{i1} \\ 1/\gamma_2 y_{i2} \\ \cdots \\ 1/\gamma_n y_{in} \end{pmatrix} \qquad (9.3)$$

where

$$s = \sum_{j=1}^{n} \bar{\phi}_j - M \qquad (9.4)$$

and

$$\eta_i = \sum_{k=1}^{n} \frac{1}{\gamma_k} \frac{1}{y_{ik}} \qquad (9.5)$$

In particular, s provides a measure of the business group capital constraint [42].

From (9.3) we have, for the j-th firm,

$$\tilde{\phi}_j^i = \bar{\phi}_j - \frac{s}{\eta_i} \frac{1}{\gamma_j} \frac{1}{y_{ij}} \qquad (9.6)$$

so that

$$\bar{\phi}_j - \tilde{\phi}_j^i = \frac{s}{\eta_i} \frac{1}{\gamma_j} \frac{1}{y_{ij}} \qquad (9.6)'$$

---

[42] While the w_j's $(j = 1, 2, \ldots, n)$ may be either positive or negative, on the contrary the v_j's, being market values, must be non-negative. Given the functional form (9.1), this condition is surely satisfied if the $\tilde{\phi}_j^i$, $j = 1, 2, \ldots, n$, are non-negative. Therefore in what follows, to keep the analysis as simple as possible, we will assume that the parameters γ_j and $\bar{\phi}_j$, for $j = 1, 2, \ldots, n$, always satisfy the condition

$$\bar{\phi}_j \gamma_j \geq \frac{s}{\eta_i} \frac{1}{y_{ij}}$$

represents a measure of the underinvestment of firm j Notice that this underinvestment originates from two distinct causes. First, the business group as a whole is capital constrained and, second, the ownership structure of the group is itself affecting the allocation of resources. We are therefore comparing two rather different arrangements for the managing of firm j, i.e. the case of a firm belonging to a capital constrained business group and the case of a non capital constrained firm run by managers who act in the best interests of the shareholders of their firm. We want now to identify the two above mentioned components of underinvestment, i.e. the shortage of capital effect and the business group effect. To this aim we will compare, as in Chapter 8, two alternative ownership structures, i.e. the group and the multidivisional. In the latter case (i.e. for $y_{ij} = y_i$, $j = 1, 2, \ldots, n$) the solution of problem (8.1) in the present framework, denoted by $\tilde{\phi}_j$, is given by

$$\tilde{\phi}_j = \bar{\phi}_j - \frac{s}{\gamma_j} \frac{1}{\gamma} \ , \quad \forall j = 1, 2, \ldots, n \tag{9.7}$$

where

$$\gamma = \sum_{k=1}^{n} \frac{1}{\gamma_k} \tag{9.8}$$

As expected in (9.7) the amount of capital allocated to firm j is independent of the identity of the investor-decision making. Let us now compare the amounts of resources allocated to j by the two different forms of ownership structure (each with the corresponding corporate governance model). Comparing (9.6) and (9.7) we have that, for each $j = 1, 2, \ldots, n$, $\tilde{\phi}_j > \tilde{\phi}_j^i$ if and only if

$$y_{ij} < y_i^* \tag{9.9}$$

where

$$y_i^* = \frac{\gamma}{\eta_i} \tag{9.10}$$

When the integrated ownership in firm j of the controlling investor is lower than the critical value y_i^*, the multidivisional form is preferable for firm j shareholders. Let us now assume that (9.9) holds for firm j, i.e. firm j shareholders *loose* from their firm being part of a business group. From (9.6) and (9.7) we obtain

$$\Delta \tilde{\phi}_j^i \equiv \tilde{\phi}_j - \tilde{\phi}_j^i = \frac{s}{\gamma_j} \left(\frac{1}{y_{ij}} \frac{1}{\eta_i} - \frac{1}{\gamma} \right) > 0 \qquad (9.11)$$

Let Δ_G be the fraction of the total underinvestment of firm j (see equation (A6)') which is consequence of the business group structure, i.e.

$$\Delta_G \equiv \frac{\Delta \tilde{\phi}_j^i}{\tilde{\phi}_j - \tilde{\phi}_j^i} \qquad (9.12)$$

From (9.6)' and (9.10) we have

$$\Delta_G = 1 - \frac{y_{ij}}{y_i^*} \qquad (9.13)$$

so that, as y_{ij} gets close to the critical value y_i^*, the fraction of the total underinvestment of firm j due to the business group structure tends to zero and, on the other hand, for values of y_{ij} much smaller than this critical value, the group structure is responsible for a significant fraction of the underinvestment of firm j.

Let us now return to the an analysis of firm j as part of the business group. Deriving $\tilde{\phi}_j^i$, as given in equation (9.6), with respect to x_{ik} and a_{lk} we obtain, for $l = 1, 2, \ldots, n$

$$\frac{\partial \tilde{\phi}_j^i}{\partial x_{ik}} = \frac{s}{\gamma_j} \frac{1}{y_{ij} \eta_i} \left(\frac{b_{kj}}{y_{ij}} - \frac{\beta_{ik}}{\eta_i} \right) \quad , \quad j = 1, 2, \ldots, n \qquad (9.14)$$

(where, as in Chapter 8, $B \equiv (I - A)^{-1}$), and

$$\frac{\partial \tilde{\phi}_j^i}{\partial a_{lk}} = y_{il} \frac{\partial \tilde{\phi}_j^i}{\partial x_{ik}} = \quad , \quad j = 1, 2, \ldots, n \qquad (9.15)$$

so that, setting $j = k$, we have

$$\frac{\partial \tilde{\phi}_j^i}{\partial x_{ij}} > 0 \quad , \quad j = 1, 2, \ldots, n \qquad (9.14)'$$

and (for $l = 1, 2, \ldots, n$)

$$\frac{\partial \tilde{\phi}^i_j}{\partial a_{lj}} > 0 \quad , \quad j = 1, 2, \ldots, n \tag{9.15}'$$

Let us now examine the effect of changes in ownership structure on actual underlying values. The latter are determined, through equation (9.1), by the choice of the controlling investor i of ϕ^i_j given by (9.3). We obtain

$$\tilde{w}^i_j = w_j(\tilde{\phi}^i_j) = \gamma_j \, \bar{\phi}^2_j - \left(\frac{s}{\eta_i}\right)^2 \frac{1}{\gamma_j} \frac{1}{y^2_{ij}} \quad , \quad j = 1, 2, \ldots, n \tag{9.16}$$

Note that, if the business group as a whole had not been capital constrained, the *optimal* potential underlying value of firm j would have been

$$\bar{w}_j = w_j(\bar{\phi}_j) = \gamma_j \, \bar{\phi}^2_j \tag{9.17}$$

which is larger than the actual underlying value given by (9.16). Obviously, this comparison is with a somehow ideal situation and only aims at constituting a suitable bench mark for the analysis.

Deriving eq. (9.16) with respect to a_{lk} and x_{ik}, after some simple algebra, we obtain

$$\frac{\partial \tilde{w}^i_j}{\partial x_{ik}} = \frac{2s^2}{\eta^2_i} \frac{1}{\gamma_j y^2_{ij}} \left(\frac{b_{kj}}{y_{ij}} - \frac{\beta_{ik}}{\eta_i} \right) \quad , \quad j = 1, 2, \ldots, n \tag{9.18}$$

and

$$\frac{\partial \tilde{w}^i_j}{\partial a_{lk}} = y_{il} \frac{\partial \tilde{w}^i_j}{\partial x_{ik}} \quad , \quad j = 1, 2, \ldots, n \tag{9.19}$$

where

$$\beta_{ik} = \sum_{s=1}^{n} \frac{1}{\gamma_s} \frac{b_{ks}}{y^2_{is}} \tag{9.20}$$

Therefore, setting $j = k$ in the above two equations, we have

$$\frac{\partial \tilde{w}^i_j}{\partial x_{ij}} > 0 \tag{9.19}'$$

and (for $l = 1, 2, \ldots, n$)

$$\frac{\partial \tilde{w}_j^i}{\partial a_{lj}} > 0 \qquad (9.20)'$$

As explained in §7.2, in a market characterized by cross-share-holdings among firms two measures of value can be defined, i.e. underlying and market values. From equations (7.3) and (7.4), the two measures of value are linked through a Leontiev type relation, so when the underlying value of firm j is given by (9.16), the corresponding market value is

$$\tilde{v}_j^i = \left(B \tilde{w}^i \right)_j$$

$$= \sum_{k=1}^n b_{jk} \gamma_k \bar{\phi}_k^2 - \frac{s^2}{\eta_i^2} \sum_{k=1}^n b_{jk} \frac{1}{\gamma_k} \frac{1}{y_{ik}^2} \qquad (9.21)$$

$$= \sum_{k=1}^n b_{jk} \gamma_k \bar{\phi}_k^2 - \frac{s^2}{\eta_i^2} \beta_{ij}$$

Note, again, that if the business group as a whole had not been capital constrained, the potential market value of firm j would have been

$$\bar{v}_j = \left(B \bar{w} \right)_j$$

$$= \sum_{k=1}^n b_{jk} \gamma_k \bar{\phi}_k^2 \qquad (9.22)$$

which is larger than the actual market value given by (9.21). Shareholders of firm j would therefore be suffering a loss for their firm being part of the business group, and this would amount, in market value terms, to

$$\Delta \tilde{v}_j^i \equiv \tilde{v}_j^i - \bar{v}_j$$

$$= \frac{s^2}{\eta_i^2} \beta_{ij} \qquad (9.23)$$

However, as explained above, the comparison must be considered with care.

The same results derived with reference to underlying values can now also be obtained for market values. Indeed, deriving eq.(9.21) with respect to x_{ik} and a_{lk} $(l = 1, 2, \ldots n)$, after some simple algebra, we obtain

$$\frac{\partial \tilde{v}_j^i}{\partial x_{ik}} = \frac{2s^2}{\eta_i^3} \left(\eta_i \theta_{ikj} - \beta_{ij} \beta_{ik} \right) \quad , \quad j = 1, 2, \ldots, n \qquad (9.24)$$

and

$$\frac{\partial \tilde{v}_j^i}{\partial a_{lk}} = b_{jl} \tilde{v}_k^i + y_{il} \frac{\partial \tilde{v}_j^i}{\partial x_{ik}} \quad , \quad j = 1, 2, \ldots, n \qquad (9.25)$$

where (for $k = 1, 2, \ldots, n$)

$$\theta_{ikj} = \sum_{s=1}^{n} \frac{b_{ks} b_j s}{\gamma_s y_{is}^3} = \theta_{ijk} \qquad (9.26)$$

so that setting $k = j$ in (9.24) and (9.25) we obtain and

$$\frac{\partial \tilde{v}_j^i}{\partial x_{ij}} > 0 \quad , \quad j = 1, 2, \ldots, n \qquad (9.24)'$$

and

$$\frac{\partial \tilde{v}_j^i}{\partial a_{lj}} > 0 \quad , \quad j = 1, 2, \ldots, n \qquad (9.25)'$$

Chapter 10

Ownership Concentration and Corporate Control

10.1 Concentrate Shareholdings and Monitoring

Corporate finance and corporate governance mechanisms differ sharply across countries. For example, in the United States and the United Kingdom firms are widely thought of as relying primarily on the threat of a takeover by outsiders to ensure that managers act in the shareholders' interest, while German and Japanese firms are thought to be governed by the banks with which they have close ties. What are the reasons for these striking differences? What are the costs and the benefits of the different mechanisms of corporate control? In this Chapter we will address these issues by describing the main characteristics of the corporate control mechanisms in large non financial firms in the United States, the United Kingdom, Japan and Germany. Moreover, we will try to shed light on the question of why these differences exist. The dominant theme of this Chapter (see also Prowse, 1994, for a similar approach) is that concentrated holdings of a firm's financial claims may be the most efficient way of resolving agency problems in firms (see, e.g., Stiglitz, 1985). The intuition is very simple. Suppose, firstly, that the equity of the firm is concentrated in the hands of a few investors. Then each investor will have sufficient private incentive to invest in information acquisition and monitoring of management. Moreover, large shareholders will be in a position to exert control over management. This can be achieved either through their voting rights or through representation on the board of directors, or both. The limited diversification which these investor can achieve is, of course, the cost of their large stakes. Suppose now that the firm's debt is concentrated in the hands of few banks or other lenders. Again, these institutions will have an incentive to engage in monitoring. There is, however, a difference. The point here is that *"lenders are only interested in the bottom part of the tail of the distribution of returns"* (Prowse, 1994, p.12), and they therefore tend to be less interested in whether the managers are maximizing the value of the firm. This problem can be mitigated to the extent that the large lenders to the firms are also large shareholders.

But is concentrate shareholding in practice a viable mechanism for disciplining managers? There are two necessary conditions for a positive answer to the above question. First, the observed patterns of corporate ownership must show the required high degree of concentration, and second, large shareholders must possess the right incentives to perform the function of active monitors. Only when both these conditions are satisfied can concentrated shareholding be an effective way for disciplining managers. In this Chapter we analyze the extent to which these conditions are satisfied in the four major industrialized countries mentioned above (the United States, the United Kingdom, Japan and Germany). However, before examining the different forms of corporate ownership and corporate control in the four countries under study, a preliminary remark is in order. The differences we observe between countries in patterns of ownership and forms of corporate governance do not appear to be simply accidents of history or culture but seem to be instead the result of striking differences in the firm's legal and regulatory environment which affects the degree to which the concentrated holding of the firm's financial claims is achieved. If, as mentioned above, concentrated holdings are important from a corporate control perspective, in the absence of such concentration alternative mechanisms of corporate control must be relied upon to ensure management discipline. Now, there are essentially two differences between the four countries under study that affect the system under which firms operate and are important determinants of corporate control mechanisms. The first is the severity of legal and regulatory constraints on large investors being *active* investors in firms, arising from differences in company and bankruptcy law, in the portfolio regulation of financial institutions, tax laws, insider trading laws, disclosure rules and antitrust laws. Historically the US and UK laws have been much more hostile to investors taking large influential stakes. For example, in the US financial institutions face significant constraints on their ability to take large stock positions in firms and use them for corporate control purposes [43]. Moreover, commercial banks are simply prohibited from owning any stock on their own account by the Glass-Steagall Act of 1933. These regulatory restrictions on investors' holdings of large debt and equity stakes in individual firms has led to relatively dispersed holdings of such claims in the Anglo-Saxon countries. Conversely, the absence of such restrictions in Japan and particularly Germany has encouraged concentrated holdings of corporate debt and equity by both financial institutions and other corporations.

The second difference in the legal and regulatory environment of the four countries which affects firms' corporate control mechanisms relates to the degree to which firms are discouraged from tapping non-bank forms of external finance by laws that directly suppress the development of domestic corporate securities markets. For example, until the mid 1980s in Japan and until very recently in Germany there have been significant obstacles facing firms wishing to raise external finance from sources other than banks. These legal and regulatory impediments to the development of securities markets have meant that firms have had to rely on banks to provide a large share of their total financing needs. This, in, turn has encouraged concentrated holdings.

10.2 Patterns of Corporate Ownership

In what follows we will first broadly classify the financial markets of major industrialized countries and then analyze the structure of corporate ownership in the US, the UK, Japan, Germany and Italy, focusing in particular on the concentration of ownership and on the identity of large shareholders. We will finally

---

[43] For a detailed description of these restrictions, see Roe, 1990, and Prowse, 1990.

examine the different corporate control mechanisms in the above countries. Special attention will be devoted to the analysis of the relationship of institutions to corporate management.

The financial systems of industrialized countries can be broadly divided in two categories, namely those relying heavily on *internal capital markets* and those endowed with well developed *external capital markets*. The term internal capital market has been widely used to refer to the allocation of capital within a large conglomerate through bureaucratic decision-making centralized in the office of the chief executive (see O.Williamson, 1975). However, the term has also been used to apply to allocation decisions made within a large group or network of firms (such as the Japanase keiretsu or the business group of Continental Europe). We use the term in that latter sense, to distinguish an internal capital market from an external capital market in which the firm has access to many active suppliers of capital. Internal capital markets are widely diffused in Japan, Germany, France and Italy, while United States and United Kingdom have highly developed external capital markets. It is interesting to notice that if we have divided the financial systems of developed countries by focusing on the relative importance of financial markets and intermediaries (as in Allen and Gale, 1995), we would end up with roughly the same partition. Indeed, following the latter criterion, at one extreme we have Germany where a few large banks play an important role and financial markets are not very important, and at the other extreme are the U.S. where financial markets play an important role and the banking industry is much less concentrated. Other developed countries, such as U.K., France, Italy and Japan are somewhere in between. So we can roughly conclude that countries in which firms heavily rely on internal capital markets are those where financial intermediation is more important and where firms tend to organize their activities in industrial groups, while countries with developed financial markets are those which depend less on banking intermediation and where firms tend to be publicly held and to look at the market for financing their investment opportunities. Of course, the classifications above are to a large extent approximate and non totally satisfactory in several respects since we know neither why different countries have developed such different financial systems, nor we fully understand the merits of different systems.

As different countries are characterized by different pattern of corporate ownership and, correspondingly, by different institutional investors, so the relationship of institutions to corporate management differs from country to country. In what follows we briefly review the pattern of corporate ownership and the position of institutional investors, beginning with the United States and United Kingdom and then moving to internal capital market economies such as Germany and Japan. A brief analysis of the situation in Italy concludes. Necessarily, the discussion of each country is incomplete and, in some respects, cursory. The intent, however, is to contrast the essentially internal capital markets that characterize Germany and Japan (and the associated essentially internal corporate control mechanisms) with the external capital markets in the U.S. and in the U.K. (and the corresponding external corporate control mechanisms). In particular, we will analyze the practices developed in the external capital market economies in order to mediate conflicts between institutional investors and corporate managers, we will assess the costs of these practices and investigate why these countries have in recent years been forced to undertake major revisions in their corporate control mechanisms.

The most relevant institutional investors in the United States in 1991 have been pension funds, holding about a quarter of publicly listed corporations, and Mutual Investment Funds, with a little less than a tenth of listed firms (Kester, 1993). As far as the total institutional holding is concerned, in 1950 institutional investors owned only 8 per cent of the equity in United States corporations. By 1980, this level had risen to 33 per cent, and by 1988, it had reached 48 per cent (Coffee, 1991). Moreover, institutional ownership is extremely heavy at the upper end of corporate America. Among the top 100 American corporations in term of stock market value, the level of institutional ownership is now at 53 per cent (and, for example, is at 82 per cent at General Motors Corp and at 74 per cent at Mobil Corp). Many institutions now hold 2-3 per cent of the stock of a single company and some hold more than 5 per cent. It has also been calculated (Lowenstein, 1991) that for the average corporation listed in the Standard & Poor's 500, it takes just twenty institutional holders to account for 34 per cent of the outstanding stock.

The British capital markets match those of the United States in being extremely active and well developed. Institutional ownership is nowadays increasing, and has long been higher in the U.K. than in the U.S. As in U.S., the most important institutional investors in the U.K. in 1991 have been pension funds, holding about a third of publicly listed corporations, while the second larger institutional investors in the British market in 1991 have been Insurance Companies, with a little less than a fifth of all listed companies (Kester, 1993). As far as the total institutional holding is concerned, British institutional ownership rose from 47 per cent in 1975 to over 60 per cent in 1991.

In 1990, the distribution of share ownership of listed Japanese corporations was as follows: financial institutions held 45.2 per cent (4.5 per cent as investment or pension trusts), domestic non-financial corporations (including securities companies) held 26.9 per cent; domestic individuals held 23.1 per cent; and foreign individuals and corporations held 4.2 per cent (Sheard, 1994). A typical listed firm in Japan has extensive interlocking shareholdings with transaction partners (banks, insurance companies, suppliers, customers trading companies, etc.) and affiliated firms. The firm, moreover, both owns shares in these firms and has a significant fraction of its shares held by these firms. The parcel of shares held may be quite small, typically around 1 per cent or less for non-financial firms and up to several per cent for financial institutions. Taken together, however, shares held in this way usually constitute a majority of the firm's issued shares.

As it has been mentioned in the Introduction, the predominant industrial organization structure in Japan is the keiretsu group. There are six major keiretsu groups today. Three of these (Mitsui, Mitsubishi and Sumitomo) are descended from the former *zaibatsu* [44], while the other three are newer groups which have formed around major banks (Fuyo-Fuji, Dai-Ichi Kangyo, and Sanwa). The internal structure of the keiretsu varies with the industry and the relationship upon which the coalition is based [45], but typically each consists of of a diversified confederation of companies clustered around a "main bank" that provides loans to the members of the group as their chief source of financing. Although the main bank in the keiretsu is usually both a shareholder and the principal creditor of the members of its constellation of companies, its position is clearly distinguishable from that of the parent company in a large American conglomerate, because the main bank is in turn owned by its subsidiaries and affiliates. In fact, as indicated above, the legal force knitting together this structure is the system of interlocking cross-ownership under which each constituent company owns from .5 to 3 per cent of the equity in each other member in the keiretsu, thereby effectively locking control within the group.

Even more than in Japan, German corporations depend upon their banking system for access to all forms of external finance. The institutional structure of the German financial system centres on the principle of the universal banking. A universal bank is free to provide a wide range of services, from commercial to investment banking, and to invest in equities in its own account. Universal

---

[44] During the early decades of the twentieth century. the zaibatsu - family owned, bank centred holding companies - expanded through both vertical integration and diversifying acquisitions. During the occupation of Japan, the American authorities liquidated the zaibatsu expecting that American-style public corporations would evolve in their absence. However, because they underestimated the power and centrality of the banks within the zaibatsu confederations, they did not insist on the liquidation of these institutions, and this omission eventually resulted in the reemergence of a looser regrouping of the former zaibatsu interests (see Viner, 1988). These successor coalitions became known as keiretsu.

[45] For example, the number of firms within a group varies widely, from the Sumitomo group's 16 to the Dai-Ichi Kangyo group's 57.

banks can hold whatever share of equity they like in any non financial corporation. Germany's stock markets have never been a significant factor in the equity raising process as companies have traditionally relied upon long term loans from their primary banks as the major source of external finance. According to Schneider-Lenné (1993) companies are the most important shareholders in Germany with about 42 per cent of all publicly listed corporations. German banks own about 10 per cent of all shares and Insurance Companies hold about 12 per cent. No other class of institutional investor has significant holdings. The overall level of institutional ownership of German corporations is, therefore, around half that in the United States.

The above reported aggregate figures of ownership of common stock in the four countries under scrutiny, however, reveal nothing about *the concentration* of ownership nor about the identity of the large shareholders in a typical firm. These features of corporate ownership are particularly relevant for the purposes of our analysis since both the degree of concentration and the identity of large shareholders are of fundamental importance to evaluate the incentives of these shareholders to engage in monitoring of management (and, correspondingly, the effectiveness of such monitoring). For example, it seems to be relevant to distinguish between shares which financial institutions hold on their own account and those they hold as agents for their investors (as, e.g., in Porter, 1992, or in Prowse, 1994). It seems reasonable to think, for a variety of reasons, that only shares held on own account are held for long-term corporate control purposes. Now, even if in aggregate in Anglo-Saxon countries the institutional ownership is considerable, however the overwhelming majority of shares held by financial institutions are held in their capacity as agents for other investors. In contrast, in Japan and Germany ownership of shares by financial institutions on their own account is very substantial [46].

---

[46] Moreover, in Germany banks have traditionally been given wide latitude to exercise the voting rights attaching to the shares they hold in trust for smaller shareholders. Therefore, in evaluating total insti-

To have a clearer picture of both the concentration of ownership and the identity of large shareholders in the four countries under scrutiny, an analysis of the ownership patterns of a sample of firms in each of those countries is required. An attempt to perform such an analysis is provided by Prowse, 1994. Using a sample of large listed US, UK, Japanese and German non-financial firms at various periods in the past two decades, Prowse shows how there are large differences in ownership concentration in the four countries under study. In his sample of firms, he finds that in both the United States and the United Kingdom the five largest shareholders hold on average between a fifth and a quarter of the outstanding shares. Ownership concentration is significantly higher in Japan (where the five largest shareholders hold on average a third of the outstanding shares), but is by far the highest in Germany where the holdings of the five largest shareholders averages over 40 per cent. Moreover, because proxy votes exercised by banks on behalf of beneficial shareholders are very important in large German corporations, the ownership concentration in Germany is probably even larger than these data suggest. In sum, in the United States and the United Kingdom ownership concentration is relatively low. This is a result, at least to a large extent, of the legal and regulatory costs documented above of taking a large, active equity position in a company (see below, however, for more on this point). Ownership concentration is somewhat higher in Japan, where the most important large shareholders are banks which therefore have the primary responsibility for monitoring management. Finally, ownership concentration is substantially higher in Germany, where majority owned firms are much more prevalent than in other countries and where the ability of banks to exercise by proxy the voting rights of small shareholders gives them a potentially powerful position in influencing management.

In part as a consequence of the differences in the legal and

---

tutional ownership in Germany we should also consider these shares (approximately 14 per cent of outstanding equity). Failing to consider these figures, would substantially alter the picture of corporate control mechanisms in Germany.

regulatory enviroment faced by firms, the different patterns of corporate ownership and ownership concentration correspond to substantially different forms of corporate governance. and mechanisms of corporate control in the four countries under study. In the US and the UK, although financial institutions own a large share of the outstanding corporate equity in the aggregate, almost all of this is held as agents for beneficial owners. These agents - pension funds, mutual funds, life insurance companies - have strong incentives from portfolio regulations and insider trading laws to keep their portfolios liquid by taking very small holdings in a wide variety of companies. Consequently ownership tends to be diffuse and, until recently, shareholder monitoring weak. Historically, external mechanisms of corporate control have been the primary means in Anglo-Saxon countries for disciplining managers [47]. However, the reliance of US and UK firms on the external markets for corporate control does not mean that the internal mechanisms of corporate control are non-existent - just that they are likely to be weaker and to act more slowly than internal mechanisms in other countries.

Corporate governance mechanisms in Germany and Japan, in contrast, strongly rely on direct shareholder monitoring. In Japan, in particular, the corporate control framework is related to the keiretsu form of corporate organization (see above). Ownership concentration is relatively high, as is the concentration of debt claims. Banks are the most important shareholders of firms and until recently they have also been their only major source of external finance. Consequently, they have a potentially very powerful position as active monitors of management either through boards or through more informal mechanisms or through their control of the firm's access to external funds. The market for corporate control among large firms is inactive. In Germany there

---

[47] In particular takeover processes have generally been considered as playing a central role in allowing control to be transferred from inefficient to efficient management. Franks and Mayer (1996), however, find little evidence that hostile takeovers are motivated by poor performance prior to bids, and they therefore reject the view that hostile takeovers performs a disciplinary role.

appears to be even more reliance on direct shareholder monitoring. Ownership concentration among large firms is high enough to give the large shareholders substantial incentive to monitor the management. Banks, in particular, appear to have the potential to engage in monitoring and influencing management, particularly in the diffusely held firms where their control of voting rights may be important. However, Edwards and Fischer (1994) argue that the evidence suggests that bank monitoring is of limited importance. The three major banks and some of the other commercial banks do appear to act in this way, but they constitute a relatively small part of the banking system. Moreover, compared with Japanese banks, German banks appear to have somewhat less control over firms through their control of external sources of finance, since German firms rely more on internally generated funds [48]. As in Japan, hostile takeovers are almost non-existent in Germany.

The analysis developed so far has shown how the reliance in a given country on a particular mechanism of corporate control is critically dependent on the nature of the legal and regulatory environment of the firm and its investors. However, legal and regulatory systems have costs, both economic and political, which may have little to do with the mechanism of corporate control which the system supports. Moreover, these costs may change over time in response to financial innovation and market developments, and if they become too great the authorities will change laws and regulations thereby affecting the dominant corporate control mechanism.

Japan is the most recent example of this phenomenon. After remaining largely inaltered until the early 1970s, the regulatory and legal structure of the Japanese financial system has been slowly changing since then, under both domestic and international pressure for reforms. The most important aspect of

---

[48] Prowse (1994) reports data on the gross funding of non-financial corporations in the U.K., Germany and Japan for the period 1970-1985. During this period, German firms have relied on internal finance (i.e. retention) for 76 per cent of their total financing needs, compared with 52 per cent for Japanese firms (and 68 per cent for British firms).

Japanese deregulation from a corporate control perspective has been the gradual and continuing removal, in the face of increasing competition from the European markets, of restrictions on non-bank finance. In response to this deregulation, the traditional ties between banks and large firms are substantially weakening in recent years. Exactly what this will imply for corporate control mechanisms is not yet clear. However, as the methods of corporate control evolve, it is likely that there will be some changes from the previous regime.

The German legal and regulatory environment has also shown signs of changing recently. In an attempt to compete with London as a financial centre, many of the restrictions on corporate finance have been relaxed. Again, it is not clear how the methods of corporate control will evolve. The US and the UK financial systems have also recently been changing. In the US the debate centres on whether the current restrictions on the ability of financial institutions to be active investors in firms are impediments to a more efficient corporate governance mechanism. Some restrictions, such the SEC's rules on shareholder activism, have already been relaxed and this has already led to some financial institution involvement in firms' decisions. How far these changes will go, is at the moment difficult to predict.

How does Italy stand with respect to the issues here discussed? The Italian model of capitalism is in many respect atypical since is not easily framed in any of the two stylized systems described above. It is neither a system centred on well developed stock markets, with several public companies and little financial intermediation (as in the Anglo-Saxon external model) nor it is a system characterized by extensive bank involvements in running firms' operations and effective financial institution supervision on corporate managers (as in the German and Japanese internal system).

In an extensive study of ownership structure and mechanisms of corporate control of large and medium Italian firms, Barca et al.(1994) find that the corporate grouping structure is so popular that almost all quoted firms are part of a pyramidal business group [49] and only 180 main business groups exercise control over 6500 firms. The degree of ownership concentration in the about 10,000 firms included in their sample is extremely high since for 67 per cent of these firms the top shareholder owns a fraction greater than 50 per cent (and the top three shareholders own together more than 71 per cent). From an international perspective, the Italian system resembles the German and Japanese model in that non financial corporations hold about 22 per cent of quoted firms. However, the holdings of institutional investors (mainly banks) is in Italy especially low since it accounts for only 12 per cent of quoted firms. Conversely, the fraction of quoted firms directly owned by the state is extremely high since it accounts for about 28 per cent of all listed companies [50]. The control of about two thirds of the Italian quoted firms is exercised through the business group form, i.e. the integrated holding of the controlling investor is less than 50 per cent but his holding through the chain of the other group's firms is altogether sufficient to exercise control.

As already mentioned (see §7.1.1 above), Italy is just about to gradually increase the importance of the private funding in retirement financing [51]. Once institutional investors will be effectively allowed to grow and operate, it seems likely (and maybe desirable) that they will channel a sizeable proportion of their money into financial markets affecting both markets' and firms' operations. However, as it has been shown in Chapter 8 (see Propositions 8.2

---

[49] Moreover, about 55 per cent of the industrial firms with more than 50 employees belong to a business group (and this percentage is increasing with the dimension of the firm).

[50] This share, however, is now shrinking as a result of the privatization program undertaken by the Government in the last two years.

[51] Before the recent agreement between the Government and the Unions to change the state pension system, state pension entitlements in Italy were the most lavish in Europe absorbing more than 40% of government expenditure In a recent study (P. van den Noord and R. Herd, 1993) it has been calculated that, without reform and at plausible rates of growth in earnings, the share of spending on state pensions in Italy would more than double between 1990 and 2040 from 11% to 23% of GDP.

- 8.3), in a market characterized by large cross-holdings the controlling investor can seriously affect the interests of minority shareholders. This raises the issue of the protection of non-controlling shareholders, which will be extensively analyzed in the next Chapter. We will compare two possible institutional behaviour, namely shareholder passivity versus activism. The analysis rests on the assumptions that international trend (growing institutional concentration, above all) and local factors (a poorly developed stock market with only a few available stocks) might induce newly established Italian institutional investors to take an active role in firms' corporate governance. This, in turn, could deeply affect the nowadays predominant forms of corporate ownership and corporate governance.

Chapter 11

Large Investor Activism and Corporate Monitoring

11.1 Introduction

As shown in the previous Chapter, the growing concentration (especially in the U.S. and in the U.K.) of institutional ownership is radically changing the nature of the relationship between managers and shareholders of large quoted companies. Historically, institutional investors dissatisfied with managerial performance simply sold their holdings, i.e. followed an "exit" policy. However, this has now become increasingly difficult for many institutions. Coffe (1991) provides an insight into the changing behaviour of institutional investors from being passive investors to active monitors. He suggests that the trend toward increased activism on the part of institutional investors can be explained by the fact that exercising "voice" has become less costly because of the significant ownership of equity by institutions and the "resulting increased capacity for collective action"; at the same time, following an "exit" policy has become increasingly more expensive because they must accept substantial discounts in order to liquidate their significant holdings [52]. In this Chapter we examine how the activism of a large shareholder (e.g. an institutional investor) could

---

[52] In particular, the above mentioned activism can be extremely valuable for institutional investors like pension funds heavily investing in index funds and for which therefore the "Wall Street rule" (i.e. dissatisfied investors sell their shares) is not viable. The use of indexation means that pension fund performance is strongly dependent on the performance of the companies making up the index. This suggests that it is in the interest of pension funds to actively monitor the companies in the index, especially those carrying a significant weight in the index. For

become an effective way to limit the power of business groups in an economy characterized by large cross-shareholdings. In particular, we argue that shareholder activism might be a response to the inefficiencies in the internal allocation of resources described in Chapter 8 and which are a direct consequence of the group's ownershp structure. We will focus on the collective action problems facing active shareholders (see Olson, 1971, and, more recently, Black, 1990). We first discuss, in §11.2, the incentives of a large institutional investor to make a stock price enhancing proposal, and we characterize the optimal amount of resources invested by the proponent in soliciting support. We then examine the incentives of non-proponent shareholders to consider and vote on the proposal. Furthermore, in section 11.3, within the framework developed in Chapter 9, we show how activism can act as device to force the investor controlling the group to take into consideration the interests of the minority shareholders in one firm of the group. Concluding remarks are provided in §11.4.

11.2 Activism and Monitoring

To decide whether and when to become active, an institutional investor compares the expected costs of a course of action with the expected benefits. The costs of activism depend primarily on the tools with which an institution exerts influence, from the high cost of waging a formal proxy fight to the low cost of holding informal discussions with management. The benefits depend partly on the probability of success and partly on the issue at hand, with more potential benefit from proposals directly af-

---

example, indexed investors, who in effect match their portfolios to market indicators, continued to be big holders of IBM, at one time a huge component of the S&P's 500, even as the computer company turned in several years of dismal financial performance. The argument for activism obviously fails if pension funds managers are evaluated only on the basis of comparisons with the index. In our analysis, however, we are assuming that institutions manage their funds in the best interests of their clients, and and we therefore abstract from potential agency problems between the money manager and the institution's board.

fecting stock price and less from proposals for procedural reforms. In what follows, to keep the analysis as simple as possible, we will examine only institutional investor proposals which can directly affect stock price. Let us consider an institutional investor holding a significant stake in a given firm (firm j from now on) belonging to a business group. As shown in Chapter 8, firm j is managed in the best interests of the group's controlling investor, and this can severely damage the interests of firm j minority shareholders. We will assume in what follows that shareholders of firm j are penalized by their firm being part of the business group. In the light of the analysis developed in Chapters 8 and 9, this is the case when, for example, the integrated ownership in firm j of the controlling investor satisfies condition (8.7), i.e. is sufficiently low to make the multidivisional form preferable for firm j non controlling shareholders. We will also assume that the actual market value of firm j, $\tilde{v}_j^i$, is lower than it would be under a different management. We will indicate this optimal potential market value of firm j by $\bar{v}_j$. For the time being (and until Proposition 11.2 below), we do not need to make any further assumption on the specific form of $\bar{v}_j$.

Under these assumptions, shareholders in firm j are suffering a loss $\Delta\tilde{v}_j^i$ in market value given by

$$\Delta\tilde{v}_j^i \equiv \bar{v}_j - \tilde{v}_j^i \qquad (11.1)$$

The institutional investor is risk neutral and owns a fraction α_I^j in firm j. We will assume that all securities of firm j have votes in the same proportion as their claim to income (one share-one vote) and we defer to Grossman and Hart (1988) for an analysis of the influence of a firm's security-voting structure on the market for corporate control. The fraction α_I^j can also be thought of as the sum of the positions of a group of several large institutional shareholders acting together. Since we are assuming a high level of concentration of institutional ownership, the generally shared objectives among this type of shareholders are likely to imply small coordination costs and therefore a considerable amount of cooperation among institutions-shareholders. We want to analyze the decision faced by the institutional investor whether to make a proposal (and so becoming active) that managers of firm j are expected to oppose. The assumption of sure managerial opposition to the institutional proposal greatly simplifies the analysis that follows and it is justified on the grounds that the managers of firm j, as mentioned above, are acting on behalf of the business group's controlling investor, and they must therefore put the interests of the whole group before those of firm j. This situation creates conflict of interests between managers and shareholders of firm j. The institutional investor-proponent must decide whether to make the proposal: if the proposal is made and it succeeds, then all the shareholders share pro-rata the benefits of the success [53]. We use the notation of Chapters 8 and 9. As mentioned above, $\Delta \tilde{v}_j^i$ is the greatest potential gain that could accrue to firm j shareholders if the managers' action were to be reversed. However, we also want to consider proposals that lead to smaller gains. In order to model this, let $\lambda \in [0,1]$ be a parameter characterizing the importance of the institutional investor's proposal, i.e. we assume that the potential gain accruing to firm j shareholders from the success of the institutional investor's proposal is equal to $\lambda \Delta \tilde{v}_j^i$. For $\lambda = 1$, shareholders would be able to capture the entire difference between potential and actual value, while low value of λ characterize proposals of more limited effectiveness. We also assume that the proponent's spending in the proposal is made up of three parts:

i) a fixed cost, c_j, borne pro rata by all shareholders of firm j for the shareholders' and managers' action on the proposal;

ii) a fixed cost, $\bar{c}_I$, incurred only by the proponent, which gives to the proposal a fixed probability of success p^0;

iii) an extra proponent's spending, c_I, which increase of $p(c_I)$ the probability of success of the proposal.

The relevant notations are summarized below:

---

[53] This assumption does not consider possible private benefits from control and the analysis that follows may be more appropriate for situations where control is not at stake (i.e. proxy fights). However, in principle, the analysis carries through even if the proposal involves directly a request of a change in control.

VALUES AND BENEFITS FROM ACTIVISM

$$\bar{v}_j = \text{firm } j \text{ potential market value}$$

$$\tilde{v}_j^i = \text{firm } j \text{ actual market value}$$

$$\Delta\tilde{v}_j^i = \text{maximum potential gain from activism}$$

$$\lambda \in [0, 1] = \text{fraction of } \Delta\tilde{v}_j^i \text{ accruing to shareholders}$$
$$\text{if proposal succeeds}$$

OWNERSHIP SHARES

$$\alpha_I^j = \text{institutional investor's fractional share ownership}$$

$$\delta^j = \text{business group's control stake}$$

$$\alpha_0^j = \text{small shareholders' fractional share ownership}$$

where

$$\delta^j = x_{ij} + \sum_{k=1}^{n} a_{kj} \tag{11.2}$$

and

$$\alpha_I^j + \alpha_0^j + \delta^j = 1 \tag{11.3}$$

COST STRUCTURE

$$\bar{c}_I = \text{proponent's fixed cost to make the proposal}$$

$$c_I = \text{proponent's extra spending in soliciting support}$$

$$c_j = \text{fixed cost borne pro rata by all shareholders}$$

$$c_0 = \text{small shareholders' cost to consider and vote}$$
$$\text{on the proposal}$$

PROBABILITIES OF SUCCESS OF THE PROPOSAL

$$p^0 = \text{probability of success if proponent incurs}$$
$$\text{only the fixed cost } \bar{c}_I$$
$$p^0 + p(c_I) = \text{probability of success if proponent incurs}$$
$$\text{also cost } c_I$$

The institutional investor will make the proposal if his private net benefits from the proposal are non-negative, i.e. if

$$B = f(\alpha_I^j, \lambda, c_j, \bar{c}_I, c_I)$$
$$= \alpha_I^j [p^0 + p(c_I)] \lambda \Delta \tilde{v}_j^i - \bar{c}_I - c_I - \alpha_I^j c_j \geq 0 \tag{11.4}$$

Assuming, as it seems reasonable, that total expected benefits to shareholders exceeds the cost incurred by the firm for manager and shareholder action, i.e.

$$[p^0 + p(c_I)] \lambda \Delta \tilde{v}_j^i > c_j \tag{11.5}$$

then it is immediately evident from (11.4) that net expected benefits to proponents are increasing in λ (important proposals will encourage activism) and in α_I^j (large institutional ownership will also encourage activism), and decreasing in c_j (high fixed costs borne by the firm discourage activism). Moreover, legal rules that shift fixed costs from proponents to the firm concerned will encourage proposals, since the fixed costs incurred by the firm are borne by proponents only pro-rata.

As mentioned above, after paying the fixed cost $\bar{c}_I$, the proponent is allowed to spend an extra amount c_I in order to enhance the probability of success of his proposal. The next Proposition analyzes the proponent's decision on how much to spend to solicit support.

PROPOSITION 11.1

Assume that the probability schedule $p(c_I)$ is smoothly increasing, twice differentiable with respect to the cost c_I incurred and satisfy

$$p''(c_I) < 0 \qquad (11.6)$$

Then the optimal institutional investor's spending proposal
i) is strictly increasing in the share ownership α_I^j;
ii) is strictly increasing in the importance of the proposal λ;

Proof: If a proposal is made, the cost incurred by the proponent is chosen to maximize his expected gain, i.e.

$$\max_{c_I} \quad \alpha_I^j \left[p^0 + p(c_I) \right] \lambda \Delta \tilde{v}_j^i - \bar{c}_I - c_I - \alpha_I^j c_j$$

The sufficient first and second order conditions with respect to c_I are

$$\alpha_I^j \lambda \Delta \tilde{v}_j^i p'(c_I) - 1 = 0 \qquad (11.7)$$

and

$$\alpha_I^j \lambda \Delta \tilde{v}_j^i p''(c_I) < 0 \qquad (11.8)$$

The assumptions on the probability schedule now guarantee that for each α_I^j there exists c_I such that (11.7) and (11.8) obtain to ensure an interior optimum. Parametrically differentiating (11.7) with respect to α_I^j we have

$$\alpha_I^j \lambda \Delta \tilde{v}_j^i p''(c_I) \frac{dc_I}{d\alpha_I^j} + \lambda \Delta \tilde{v}_j^i p'(c_I) = 0$$

i.e.

$$\frac{dc_I}{d\alpha_I^j} = -\frac{1}{\alpha_I^j} \frac{p'}{p''} > 0 \qquad (11.9)$$

which proves i). A similar argument also proves that c_I is strictly increasing with λ.

The results of the above Proposition seem to suggest that important proposals will be highly financed, and will therefore have high probability of success, and that large institutional ownership will also increase willingness to be active.

Until now we have analyzed the decision of an institutional investor (or a group of institutional investors acting together) who is considering whether to make a proposal that could enhance firm j stock price. However, if a large investor has made a proposal, how will the other shareholders react? In order to answer this question, notice first that we have already assumed that the investor controlling the business group (which in turn controls firm j) will oppose the proposal. Since, also by assumption, the control stake δ^j of the group in firm j is large but not enough to grant him the majority of the votes, we need to consider the remaining $\alpha_0^j = 1 - \alpha_I^j - \delta^j$ fraction of firm j shares. A part of this fraction will surely be made up of very small shareholders (i.e. families) who hold such a tiny stake in the firm to know that their vote probably will not decisive anyway. And since becoming informed is costly, they will stay uninformed, and they either will not vote at all or perhaps they will adopt a crude rule of thumb like "always vote with the management". If such rational apathy was universal and the natural default rule was "vote with management", the proponent's position would be hopeless, the managers' control of the vote absolute. As reported by Black, 1990, apathy is consistent with evidence that various antitakeover actions, even if they have a significant negative impact on stock price, nonetheless are approved by shareholders (see also Jarrel, Brickley and Netter, 1988, and Malatesta and Walking, 1988). However, apathy is not the only option for small shareholders. A considerable part of the remaining α_0^j fraction of firm j shares will be made up of banks, other corporate groups not involved in the control of firm j, and also of other institutional investors not associated with the proponent (insurance companies, investment funds, mutual funds). Even if each of these investors has a small percentage of firm j shares, nonetheless he recognizes that his vote might be decisive in order to determine the outcome of the voting on the proposal. In other words, shareholders realize that they cannot entirely free ride on the effort of others. The point was first recognized by Stigler, 1974, and more recently Holmstrom and Nalebuff, 1992, have also made a similar point concerning the solution of the classical Grossman and Hart (1980) free-rider problem in a take-over bid: the possibility of being pivotal is crucial. Following Stigler, 1974, consider the decision of a small shareholder (shareholder p, say) holding a fraction α_{0p}^j of firm j who is considering whether to incur the cost of considering and voting on the proposal. The analysis will be highly simplified, since we assume that shareholders are fully and symmetrically informed so that, if they vote, they will vote for the institutional investor's proposal (i.e. there is no divergence of opinions on expected benefits). Furthermore, if the proposal is rejected, shareholders get no benefits at all (i.e. the investor controlling the group is not expected to make any stock price enhancing restructuring or alike). Finally, for simplicity, we will also assume that the cost c_j for voting the proposal borne by firm j (i.e. by each shareholder in proportion of the shares held) is equal to zero. This is without loss of generality, since this cost is always incurred given that a proposal has been made. Let

$$\pi_v^p = \text{prob. of proposal's success if } p \text{ votes}$$

$$\pi_{nv}^p = \text{prob. of proposal's success if } p \text{ does not vote}$$

$$c_{0p} = \text{cost for } p \text{ of considering and voting the proposal}$$

where $\pi_v^p > \pi_{nv}^p$. Then the shareholder will vote if

$$\pi_v^p \left[\alpha_{0p}^j \left(p^0 + p(c_I) \right) \lambda \Delta \tilde{v}_j^i - c_{0p} \right] > \pi_{nv}^p \left[\alpha_{0p}^j \left(p^0 + p(c_I) \right) \lambda \Delta \tilde{v}_j^i \right]$$

i.e. if

$$\left(\pi_v^p - \pi_{nv}^p \right) \left[\alpha_{0p}^j \left(p^0 + p(c_I) \right) \lambda \Delta \tilde{v}_j^i \right] > \pi_v^p c_{0p} \tag{11.10}$$

i.e. the shareholder will consider the proposal if the increase in the probability of the approval of the proposal times his expected gain from the proposal if it is approved is greater than the expected cost of participating to the voting. Clearly, if the shareholder considers the probability of success totally unaffected by his vote, he will not incur the cost of considering the proposal.

From the above analysis we know that the institutional investor makes the proposal only if his net expected benefits are non-negative. However, it would be socially optimal for the proponent to make a proposal whenever the expected total benefits to all shareholders exceeds the total cost of the proposal, i.e. when

$$(p^0 + p(c_I))\lambda\Delta\tilde{v}_j^i - \bar{c}_I - c_I - c_j - c_0 > 0$$

In fact, as suggested by Black, 1990, some socially beneficial proposals will not be made because the proponent's net expected benefits are negative. More precisely, a socially beneficial proposal will not carried out by institutional investors when we have simultaneously negative net private benefits to proponents and positive net benefits to all shareholders

$$\alpha_I^j(p^0 + p(c_I))\lambda\Delta\tilde{v}_j^i - \bar{c}_I - c_I - \alpha_I^j c_j < 0$$

and

$$(p^0 + p(c_I))\lambda\Delta\tilde{v}_j^i - \bar{c}_I - c_I - c_j - c_0 > 0$$

i.e. when total expected benefits and cost structure satisfy

$$(\bar{c}_I + c_I) + c_0 + c_j < (p^0 + p(c_I))\lambda\Delta\tilde{v}_j^i < (\bar{c}_I + c_I)/\alpha_I^j + c_j$$

Missed socially beneficial proposals can therefore exist if and only if

$$\frac{c_0}{\bar{c}_I + c_I} < \frac{1 - \alpha_I^j}{\alpha_I^j} \qquad (11.11)$$

In particular, if institutional investor's per share total spending to make the proposal, $(c_I + \bar{c}_I)/\alpha_I^j$, are greater than the small shareholders' per share cost of considering it, c_0/α_0, then some socially beneficial proposals will not be made.

11.3 Activism and Business Groups

We now investigate further the conditions capable of generating institutional activism. As already mentioned, an institutional investor will make a proposal as long as his private net expected benefits from making the proposal are non-negative, i.e. (11.4) holds. An interesting issue is then to determine the share of a public firm belonging to a business group that institutional investors should try to hold in order to receive non-negative net expected benefits from activism. We will now address the above issue under the assumption of a quadratic approximation to the function w_j of the underlying value of firm j (see Chapter 9, equation (9.1)). In this framework, the market value of firm j is lower than it could be in the case of a non capital constrained firm run by managers acting in the best interests of their shareholders, and (11.1) reduces to (9.23) in Chapter 9. From (11.4) we have that, if (11.5) is satisfied, benefits from activism are non-negative when

$$\alpha_I^j \geq \bar{\alpha}_I^j = \frac{c_j}{(p^0 + p(c_I))\lambda\Delta\tilde{v}_j^i - (c_I + \bar{c}_I^j)} \qquad (11.12)$$

The following Proposition analyzes (admittedly under rather restrictive assumptions) how the above derived critical fraction of ownership is affected by changes in the group's ownership structure not followed by a change in control.

PROPOSITION 11.2

Consider a capital constrained hierarchical business group, consisting of n firms, and a particular firm belonging to the group (say, firm j). Assume (see Chapter 9) that the function w_j describing the underlying value of firm j ($j = 1, 2, \ldots, n$) is given by (A1), so that (11.1) reduces to (9.23). Moreover, assume that the overall cost structure of activism, $(c_I, \bar{c}_I, c_j)$ (and therefore also the probability of success of a proposal), is independent of the group's ownership structure, (x_i, A), and let $\bar{\alpha}_I^j$, as given in eq.(11.12), be the critical fraction of shares of firm j which make non-negative the net benefits from activism. Then

i) an increase in the controlling investor's direct holding in firm j (obtained through a purchasing of firm j shares from the market, i.e. from individual investors or firms not belonging to the group) will increase $\bar{\alpha}_I^j$.

ii) an increase in the fraction a_{lj} of firm j owned by firm l (obtained through a purchasing of firm j shares by firm l from the market) will increase $\bar{\alpha}_I^j$ if (and only if) the integrated ownership y_{il} of the controlling investor i in firm l ($l = 1, 2, \ldots n$), satisfies the condition

$$y_{il} > y_{il}^* \qquad (11.13)$$

where

$$y_{il}^* = -\frac{b_{jl}(\Delta\tilde{v}_j^i)}{\partial\Delta\tilde{v}_j^i/\partial x_{ij}} \qquad (11.14)$$

Proof: see Appendix.

The results of the above Proposition indicate how institutional investor activism can be an effective way of limiting the power of a controlling investor in a business group. First, from part i), when the investor controlling the group increases his direct holdings in firm j, firm j gets a larger fraction of the resources available within the group (see Chapter 8), so that his actual market value increases and gets closer to his optimal value. At the same time institutional activism is discouraged, since net expected benefits from proposals decrease. Second, from part ii), when the controlling investor has a sufficiently large integrated stake in firm l (i.e. firm l is an important element of the business group), then the purchasing of firm j shares by firm l from the market increases the weight of firm j within the group, with a corresponding reduction in $\Delta\tilde{v}_j^i$ which, again, makes activism more difficult. In sum, for firm j shareholders both an increase in the controlling investor's direct holding in their firm and a purchasing of their shares by an important firm of the controlling group are good news, and institutional activism can be an effective way to force these beneficial changes.

11.4 Conclusion

Industrial groups are common across Continental Europe and Japan. In particular, the hierarchical group (predominant in Continental Europe) is characterized by large cross-shareholdings between firms, well developed internal capital markets, and unitary control, often exercised through one holding company. In this Section of the book we have analyzed the influence of ownership structure on investment allocation decisions in a hierarchical group. We have first set out a model which describes the functioning of a hierarchical group, focusing in particular on the task of allocating the resources to the various member firms. In our model, this function is performed by the controlling investor, who distributes the available capital in accordance with his own interests in the various firms. This seems to be a characteristic peculiar to the hierarchical form of grouping, where moreover the share of residual claims on a group's assets held by the controlling investor may be rather small, so granting to the controller large power and authority with a limited capital. We have then compared the structure of ownership and corporate governance in a hierarchical group with those of a multidivisional firm and have established conditions which make the latter preferable for minority shareholders. As it might be expected, minority shareholders should prefer the group form only when the integrated ownership of the controlling investor is sufficiently high. We have found the critical value of integrated ownership of the controller which makes minority shareholder just indifferent between having their firm run as part of a group and as a division of a multidivisional firm. We have also showed how the controlling investor can seriously affect the interests of the minority shareholders and, in particular, we have analyzed how changes in the group's ownership structure (not followed by changes in control) affect the loss incurred by minority shareholders for their firm being part of the group.

The issue of the protection of minority shareholders seems to be a particularly important topic in these days in Italy where, as a consequence of a change in the pension system, pension funds have only recently been allowed to grow and operate in the stock market. In order to examine the possible impact of institutional investors in a market characterized by large interlocking shareholdings, in the second part of this Section we have analyzed the conditions that could induce newly established institutional investors to take an active part in firms' corporate governance, and we have then shown how institutional activism could become an effective way to limit the power of the controlling investor in a business group. If this is true, institutional investors may in the future reshape the currently predominant form of corporate governance and corporate ownership in several countries (Italy included) where external capital markets are still poorly developed.

Appendix

Proof of Proposition 11.2

Deriving $\Delta\tilde{v}_j^i$ as given in (9.23) with respect to x_{ik} and a_{lk} $(l, k = 1, 2, \ldots n)$, using the notation of Chapter 9 and after some simple algebra, we obtain

$$\frac{\partial\Delta\tilde{v}_j^i}{\partial x_{ik}} = \frac{2s^2}{\eta_i^3}\left(\beta_{ij}\beta_{ik} - \eta_i\theta_{ikj}\right) \quad , \quad j = 1, 2, \ldots, n \qquad (A11.1)$$

and

$$\frac{\partial\Delta\tilde{v}_j^i}{\partial a_{lk}} = b_{jl}\Delta\tilde{v}_k^i + y_{il}\frac{\partial\Delta\tilde{v}_j^i}{\partial x_{ik}} \quad , \quad j = 1, 2, \ldots, n \qquad (A11.2)$$

so that setting $k = j$ in (A11.1) and (A11.2) we obtain

$$\frac{\partial\Delta\tilde{v}_j^i}{\partial x_{ij}} = \frac{2s^2}{\eta_i^3}\left(\beta_{ij}^2 - \eta_i\theta_{ijj}\right) \qquad (A11.1)'$$

and

$$\frac{\partial\Delta\tilde{v}_j^i}{\partial a_{lj}} = b_{jl}\Delta\tilde{v}_j^i + y_{il}\frac{\partial\Delta\tilde{v}_j^i}{\partial x_{ij}} \qquad (A11.2)'$$

Now, from (9.24)' it follows immediately that $\Delta\tilde{v}_j^i$ is a strictly decreasing function of the controlling investor's direct holdings in firm j. Therefore, since

$$\frac{\partial\bar{\alpha}_I^j}{x_{ij}} = -\left(\frac{1}{(\bar{\alpha}_I^j)^2}\lambda(p^0 + p(c_I))\frac{\partial\Delta\tilde{v}_j^i}{\partial x_{ij}}\right) \qquad (A11.3)$$

from (A11.1)' we have that i) holds true. Furthermore, since also

$$\frac{\partial\bar{\alpha}_I^j}{a_{lj}} = -\left(\frac{1}{(\bar{\alpha}_I^j)^2}\lambda(p^0 + p(c_I))\frac{\partial\Delta\tilde{v}_j^i}{\partial a_{lj}}\right) \qquad (A11.4)$$

from (A11.2)' we have that ii) is also satisfied.

References

Aharony , J. and I. Swary, 1980, Quarterly dividend and earnings announcements and stockholders' returns: an empirical analysis, *Journal of Finance*, 35 (1), pp. 1-12.

Ali, A.. and P. Zarowin, 1992, Permanent versus transitory components of annual earnings and estimation error in earnings response coefficients, *Journal of Accounting and Economics*, 15 (2/3), pp. 249-264.

Allen, F., and D. Gale, 1995, A welfare comparison of intermediaries and financial markets in Germany and in the US, *European Economic Review*, 39, pp. 179-209.

Allen, F. and R. Michaly, 1994, Dividend Policy, in *North-Holland Handbooks of Operations Research and Management Science: Finance*, edited by R. A. Jarrow, V. Maksimovic and W. T. Ziemba.

Anderson , B.D.O. and J.B. Moore, 1979, *Optimal filtering*, Englewood Cliffs: Prentice–Hall.

Aoki, M., 1988, *Information, Incentives and Bargaining in the Japanese Economy*, Cambridge (Massachusetts), CUP.

Bajaj , M. and A. Vihjh, A., 1990, Dividend clienteles and the information content of dividend changes , *Journal of Financial Economics*, 26, pp. 193-219.

Baldone, S., F. Brioschi and S. Paleari, 1994, Ownership Measures Among Firms Connected by Cross-Shareholdings and a Further Analogy with Input-Output Theory, mimeo, Politecnico di Milano.

Ball, R. and R.L. Watts, 1972, Some time series properties of accounting income, *Journal of Finance*, 27 (3), pp. 663-681.

Barca, F., M. Bianchi, F. Brioschi, L. Buzzacchi, P. Casavola, L. Filippa, M. Pagnini, 1994, *Assetti Proprietari e Mercato delle Imprese - Vol II - Gruppo, Proprietá e Controllo nelle Imprese Medio-Grandi*, Il Mulino, Bologna.

Barsky, R. and J.B. De Long., 1993, Why does the stock market fluctuate?, *Quarterly Journal of Economics*, CVIII, 2, pp. 291-311.

Beales, H., R. Craswell and S. Salop, 1981, The efficient regulation of consumer information, *Journal of Law and Economics*, 24 (3), pp. 491-540.

Berle, A.A. and G.C. Means 1932, *The Modern Corporation and Private Property*, New York, MacMillan.

Bhattacharya, S., 1979, Imperfect information, dividend policy and the bird in the hand fallacy, *Bell Journal of Economics*, 10 (1), pp. 259-270.

Black, B., 1990, Shareholder Passivity Reexamined, *Michigan Law Review*, 89, pp. 520-608.

Blanchard, O.J. and M. Watson, 1982, Bubbles, Rational Expectations and Financial Markets, NBER WP No. 945.

Box, G.E.P. and G.M. Jenkins, 1976, *Time Series Analysis: Forecasting and Control*, Holden Day.

Bray, M. and G. Marseguerra, 1996, Dividend Policy and Excess Volatility of Stock Prices, Quaderni dell'Istituto di Econometria e Matematica dell'Università Cattolica di Milano, n. 4, May.

Brealey, R. and S. Myers, 1992, *Principles of Corporate Finance*, McGraw Hill Inc..

Brioschi, F., L. Buzzacchi and M.G. Colombo, 1989, Risk Capital Financing and the Separation of Ownership and Control in Business Groups, *Journal of Banking and Finance*, vol. 13, pp. 747-772.

Brioschi, F., L. Buzzacchi and M.G. Colombo, 1990, *Gruppi di Imprese e Mercato Finanziario*, La Nuova Italia Scientifica, Roma.

Brioschi, F., L. Buzzacchi and M.G. Colombo, 1991, More on Stock Market Value with Reciprocal Ownership, *Financial Analysts Journal*, May-June, pp. 76-78.

Bulkley, G and I. Tonks, 1989, Are U.K. stock prices excessively volatile? Trading rules and variance bounds tests *The Economic Journal*, 99, pp. 1083-1098.

Buzzacchi, L. and M. G. Colombo , 1996, Businees Groups and the Determinants of Corporate Ownership, *Cambridge Journal of Economics*, forthcoming.

Buzzacchi, L. and M. Pagnini, 1994, I Meccanismi di Funzionamento dei Circuiti Interni dei Capitali: Un'Indagine Empirica del Caso Italiano, Bank of Italy working paper.

Buzzacchi, L. and M. Pagnini, 1995, Diritti di Proprietá e Mercati Interni dei Capitali nel Modello di Impresa Italiana, *L'Industria*, n.3.

Campbell, J.Y. and R. Shiller, 1987, Cointegration and tests of present value models *Journal of Political Economy,* 95, pp. 1062-1088.

Chow, G. C., 1975, *Analysis and control of dynamic economic systems*, John Wiley.

Cochrane, J.H., 1991, Volatility tests and efficient markets *Journal of Monetary Economics,* 27, pp. 463-485.

Cochrane, J.H., 1994, Permanent and transitory component of GNP and stock prices, *Quarterly Journal of Economics,* CIX, No.1, pp. 241-265

Coffee, J. , 1991, Liquidity versus Control: The Institutional Investor as Corporate Monitor, *Columbia Law Review*, Vol. 91, pp. 1277-1368.

Darrough, M.N. and N.M. Stoughton, 1990, Financial disclosure policy in an entry game , *Journal of Accounting and Economics*, 12, pp. 219-243.

DeAngelo, H., and L. DeAngelo, 1989, Dividend policy and financial distress: an empirical investigation of troubled NYSE firms, unpublished manuscript, July.

DeAngelo, H., DeAngelo, L., and D.J. Skinnert, 1994, Reversal of fortune: Dividend policy and the disappearance of sustained earnings growth, mimeo.

DeBondt, W.F., and R. Thaler, 1985, Does the stock market overreact?, *Journal of Finance,* 40, pp. 793-808.

DeBondt, W.F., and R. Thaler, 1987, Further Evidence on Investor Overreaction and Stock Market Seasonality, *Journal of Finance,* 42, pp. 557-581.

DeGroot, M.H., 1970 *Optimal Statistical Decisions,* McGraw-Hill.

DeJong, D.N. and C.H. Whiteman, 1991, The temporal stability of dividends and stock prices: Evidence from the likelihood function, *American Economic Review,* 81, pp. 600-617.

De Long, J.B., A. Shleifer, L.H. Summers and R.J. Waldmann, 1990, Noise Trader Risk in Financial Markets, *Journal of Political Economy,* 98, pp. 703-738.

De Long, J.B., A. Shleifer, L.H. Summers and R.J. Waldmann, 1991, The Survival of Noise Traders in Financial Markets *Journal of Business,* 64, pp. 1-19.

Diamond, D. 1985, Optimal release of information by firms, *Journal of Finance,* 40 (4), pp. 1071-1094.

Divecha, A. and D. Morse, 1983, Market responses to dividend increases and changes in payout ratios, *Journal of Financial and Quantitative Analysis,* 18 (2), pp. 163-173.

Dore, R., 1986, *Flexible rigidities: industrial policy and structural adjustment in the Japanese economy 1970-1980,* Stanford University Press.

Dreze, J.H., 1985, (Uncertainty and) The firm in general equilibrium theory, *The Economic Journal,* 95, pp. 1-20.

Eddy, A. and B. Seifert, 1988, Firm Size and Dividend Announcements, *Journal of Financial Research,* 11, pp. 295-302.

Edwards, J. and K. Fischer, 1994, *Banks, finance and investment in Germany,* Cambridge University Press.

Ellerman, D., 1991, Cross-ownership of Corporations: A new Application of Input-Output Theory, *Metroeconomica,* vol. 42, pp. 33-46.

Fama, E.F., 1970, Efficient capital markets: A review of theory and empirical work, *Journal of Finance,* 25, pp. 383-417.

Fama, E.F., 1976, *Foundations of Finance, NY: Basic Books.*

Fama, E.F., 1991, Efficient capital markets: II, *Journal of Finance,* 46, 5, pp. 1575-1617.

Fama, E. F., and H. Babiak, 1968, Dividend policy: an empirical analysis, *Journal of the American Statistical Association,* 63 (324), pp. 1132-1161.

Fama, E.F., L., Fisher, M. Jensen and R. Roll, 1968, The adjustment of stock price to new information, *International Economics Review,* 10, pp. 1-31.

Fedenia, M., J.E. Hodder, A.J. Triantis, 1994, Cross-Holdings: Estimation Issues, Biases and Distortions, *The Review of Financial Studies,* Spring, pp. 61-96.

Fisher, S. and R. Merton, 1984, *Macroeconomics and finance: The role of the stock market,* Carnegie–Rochester Conference Series on Public Policy, Vol. 21.

Fishman, M.J. and K.M. Hagerty, 1989, Disclosure decisions by firms and the competition for price efficiency *Journal of Finance,* 44 (3), pp. 633-646.

Flath, D., 1992, Indirect Shareholding within Japan's Business Groups, *Economic Letters,* 38, pp. 223-227.

Flavin, M.A., 1983, Excess volatility in the financial markets: A reassessment of the empirical evidence *Journal of Political Economy,* October, pp. 929-56.

Franks, J. and C. Mayer, 1996, Hostile takeovers and the correction of managerial failure, *Journal of Financial Economics*, 40, pp. 163-181.

French, K.R., and R. Roll, 1986, Stock Return Variances: The Arrival of Information and the Reaction of Traders, *Journal of Financial Economics*, 17, pp. 5-26.

Friedman, M., 1953, The Case for Flexible Exchange Rates, *Essays in Positive Economics*, Chicago, University of Chicago Press.

Friedman, B.M., 1979, Optimal Expectations of the extreme information assumptions of "Rational Expectations" macromodels, *Journal of Monetary Economics*, 5, pp. 23-41.

Gilles, C. and LeRoy, S., 1991, Econometric aspects of the variance bounds tests: A survey *The Review of Financial Studies*, Vol. 4, 4, pp. 753-791.

Gonedes, N.J, 1978, Corporate signalling, external accounting, and capital market equilibrium: evidence on dividends, income, and extraordinary items, *Journal of Accounting Research*, 16 (1), pp. 26-79.

Grossman, S. and O. Hart, 1980, Takeover Bids, the Free Rider Problem, and the Theory of the Corporation, *Bell Journal of Economics*, 11, pp. 42-64.

Grossman, S. and O. Hart, 1988, One Share-One Vote and the Market for Corporate Control *Journal of Financial Economics*, 20, pp. 175-202.

Grossman,, S.J. and R. Shiller, 1981, The determinants of the variability of stock market prices, *American Economic Review*, 71, pp. 222-227.

Harvey, A., 1989, *Forecasting, structural time series models and the Kalman filter*, Cambridge University Press.

Healy, P.M. and K.G. Palepu, 1988, Earnings information conveyed by dividend initiations and omissions, *Journal of Financial Economics*, 21 (2), pp. 149-176.

Holmstrom, B. and B. Nalebuff, 1992, To the Raider Goes the Surplus? A Reexamination of the Free-Rider Problem, *Journal of Economics and Management Strategy*, Vol. 1, 1, Spring, pp. 37-62.

Jarrel, Brickley and Netter, 1988, The Market for Corporate Control: The Empirical Evidence Since 1980, *Journal of Economic Perspective*, 49, pp. 59-62.

Jensen, M. 1986, Agency costs of free cash flow, corporation finance and takeovers, *American Economic Review*, 76 (2), pp. 323-329.

John, K. and J. Williams, 1985, Dividends, dilution and taxes: a signalling equilibrium, *Journal of Finance*, 40 (4), pp. 1053-1070.

Kester, W.C., 1993, Industrial Groups as a System of Corporate Governance, *Oxford Review of Economic Policy*, Vol. 8, 3, pp. 24-44.

Kleidon, A., 1986a, Variance bounds tests and stock price valuation models *Journal of Political Economy*, XCIV, pp. 953-1001.

Kleidon, A., 1986b, Bias in small sample tests of stock price rationality *Journal of Business*, 59, pp. 237-61.

Kurz, M., 1994a, On Rational Beliefs Equilibria, *Economic Theory*, 4, pp. 859-876.

Kurz, M., 1994b, On the Structure and Diversity of Rational Beliefs, *Economic Theory*, 4, pp. 877-900.

Kurz, M., 1994c, Explaining volatility and excess returns, mimeo, Stanford University, California.

Kurz, M., 1994d, Asset Prices with Rational Beliefs, CEPR Publication No. 375, Stanford University, California.

Lang, L. and R. Litzenberger, 1989, Dividend announcements: cash flow signalling *vs.* free cash flow hypothesis, *Journal of Financial Economics*, 24 (1), pp. 181-192.

LeRoy, S.F., 1989, Efficient capital markets and martingales, *Journal of Economic Literature,* 27, pp. 1583-1621.

LeRoy, S.F. and R.D. Porter, 1981, The present value relation: Tests based on implied variance bounds, *Econometrica,* 49, pp. 555-574.

Lintner, J., 1956, Distribution of income of corporations among dividends, retained earnings and taxes, *American Economic Review Papers and Proc.,* 46(2), pp. 97-113.

Lowenstein, L., 1991, *Sense and Nonsense in Corporate Finance,* Reading, Massachusetts, Addison-Wesley.

Malatesta, P.H. and R. Walkling, 1988, Poison Pill Securities: Stockholder Wealth, Profitability and Ownership Structure *Journal of Financial Economics,* Vol. 20, January-March, pp. 347-76.

Marsh, T. and R. Merton, 1986, Dividend variability and variance bounds tests for the rationality of stock market prices, *American Economic Review,* 76, pp. 483-498.

Marsh, T. and R. Merton, 1987, Dividend behaviour for the aggregate stock market, *Journal of Business,* 60, pp. 1-40.

Merton, R.C., 1987a, A simple model of capital market equilibrium with incomplete information, *Journal of Finance,* 42 (3), pp. 483-510.

Merton, R.C., 1987b, On the current state of the stock market rationality hypothesis, in *Macroeconomics and Finance: Essays in honour of Franco Modigliani,* Dornbush, R., Fisher, S. and Bossons, J. (eds), Cambridge, MA: MIT Press.

Miller, M., 1986, Can management use dividends to influence the value of the firm? in *The revolution in corporate finance,* edited by Stern and Chew.

Miller, M., 1987, The informational content of dividends, in *Macroeconomics and Finance: Essays in honour of Franco Modigliani,* edited by R. Dornbush, Fisher, S. and Bossons, J., Cambridge, MA: MIT Press.

Miller, M. and F. Modigliani, 1961, Dividend policy, growth and the valuation of shares, *Journal of Business*, 34, pp. 411-433.

Miller, M. and K. Rock, 1985, Dividend policy under asymmetric information, *Journal of Finance*, 40 (4), pp. 1031-1051.

Mills, T.C., 1993, *The econometric modelling of financial time series*, Cambridge University Press.

Modigliani, F. and M. Miller, 1958, The Cost of Capital, Corporation Finance, and the Theory of Investments, *American Economic Review,* June, pp. 261-297.

Murata, Y., 1977, *Mathematics for Stability and Optimization of Economic Systems*, Academic Press, New York.

Myers, S. C. and N.S. Majluf, 1984, Corporate financing and investment decisions when firms have information that investors do not have, *Journal of Financial Economics*, 13 (2), pp. 187-221.

Nikaido, H., 1970, *Introduction to Sets and Mappings in Modern Economics*, North-Holland, Amsterdam.

van den Noord, P. and R. Herd, 1993, Pension Liabilities in the Seven Major Economies, OECD Economics Department Working paper, Paris.

Ofer, A.R. and D. Siegel, 1987, Corporate financial policy, information and market expectations: An empirical investigation of dividends, *Journal of Finance*, 42 (4), pp. 889-911.

Olson, M. , 1971, *The Logic of Collective Action: Public Goods and the Theory of Groups*, Harvard University Press, Cambridge, MA.

Pettit, R.R., 1972, Dividend announcements, security performance, and capital market efficiency, *Journal of Finance*, 27 (5), pp. 993-1007.

Porter, M.E., 1992, Capital changes: changing the ways America invests in industry, Washington D.C., Council on competitiveness, Boston, Harvard Business School Press.

Prowse, S.D., 1990, Institutional investment patterns and corporate financial behaviour in the United States and Japan, *Journal of Financial Economics*, 27 (1), pp. 43-66.

Prowse, S.D., 1994, Corporate governance in an international perspective, BIS Economic papers, No. 41, July.

Roe, M., 1990, Political and legal restraints on ownership and control of public companies, *Journal of Financial Economics*, 2 (1), pp. 7-43.

Sargent, T., 1993, *Bounded Rationality in Macroeconomics*, Oxford, Clarendon Press.

Schneider-Lenné, E.R., 1993, Corporate Control in Germany, *Oxford Review of Economic Policy*, Vol. 8, n.3, pp. 11-23.

Sheard, P., 1994, Interlocking Shareholdings and Corporate Governance, in *The Japanese Firm*, M. Aoki and R. Dore (eds), Oxford University Press, Oxford.

Shiller, R., 1979, The volatility of long-term interest rates and expectations models of the term structure *Journal of Political Economy,* 87, pp. 1190-1209.

Shiller, R., 1981, Do stock price move too much to be justified by subsequent changes in dividends ?, *American Economic Review,* 71, pp. 421-436.

Shiller, R., 1984, Stock prices and Social Dynamics, *Brookings Papers on Economic Activity,* pp. 457-498.

Shiller, R., 1987, Investor Behaviour in the October 1987 Stock Market Crash: Survey Evidence, Working Paper, Cowles Foundation, Yale University.

Shiller, R., 1989, *Market volatility* , Cambridge MA, MIT Press.

Spence, A.M., 1973, Job market signalling, *Quarterly Journal of Economics*, 87, pp. 355-374.

Stigler, G., 1974, Free Riders and Collective Action: An Appendix to Theories of Economic Regulation, *Bell Journal of Economics and Management Science*, pp. 359-365.

Stiglitz, J.E., 1985, Credit markets and the control of capital, *Journal of Money, Credit and Banking*, 17 (2), pp. 133-52.

Timmermann, A., 1993, How learning in financial markets generates excess volatility and predictability in stock prices, *Quarterly Journal of Economics*, CVIII, No.4, pp. 1135-1145.

Timmermann, A., 1994, Can Agents Learn to Form Rational Expectations? Some Results on Convergence and Stability of Learning in the U.K. Stock Market, *The Economic Journal*, 104, 425, pp. 777-797.

Tirole,, J., 1985, Asset Bubbles and Overlapping Generations, *Econometrica*, 53, pp. 1071-1100.

Verrecchia, R.E., 1983, Discretionary disclosure,*Journal of Accounting and Economics*, 5, pp. 179-194.

Verrecchia, R.E., 1990, Endogenous proprietary costs through firm interdependence, *Journal of Accounting and Economics*, 12, pp. 245-250.

Viner, A., 1988, *Inside Japanese Financial Markets.*

Wang, 1994, A model of competitive stock trading volume, *Journal of Political Economy*, 102 (1), pp. 127-168.

Watts, R., 1973, The information content of dividends, *Journal of Business*, 46 (2), pp. 191-211.

Watts, R.L. and R.W. Leftwich, 1977, The time series of annual accounting earnings, *Journal of Accounting Research*, 15 (2), pp. 253-271.

West, K.D., 1988, Bubbles, fads and stock price volatility tests: A partial evaluation *Journal of Finance*, XLIII, No. 3, pp. 636-656.

Williamson, O.E., 1975, *Markets and Hierarchies: Analysis of Antitrust Implications*, Free Press, New York.

Woolridge, J.R. and C. Gosh, 1986, Dividend cuts: do they always signal bad news? in *The revolution in corporate finance*, Stern and Chew (eds).

Druck: Strauss Offsetdruck, Mörlenbach
Verarbeitung: Schäffer, Grünstadt